the origin is pure

FIND THE DIVINE WITHIN

Venerable Master Miao Tsan

bright sky press

HOUSTON, TEXAS

bright sky press
HOUSTON, TEXAS

2365 Rice Boulevard, Suite 202,
Houston, Texas 77005

Library of Congress Cataloging-in-Publication Data on file with publisher.

Original Zen poetry at chapter open and close © 2011 by Master Miao Tsan
Translated by Jay L. Gao and Chao-Hsui Chen in collaboration
with MasterWord Services, Inc.

10 9 8 7 6 5 4 3 2 1

ISBN 978-1-936474-15-8 (softcover)

Editorial Direction, Lucy Chambers; Creative Direction, Ellen Cregan
Printed in China through Asia Pacific Offset

Master Your Mind.

Master Your Life.

the origin is pure

ACKNOWLEDGEMENTS

A book is a collaborative effort, and I have many people to acknowledge for their contributions.

Jay Gao, Chao-Hsiu Chen, and Larry Payne translated the manuscript from Chinese to English in collaboration with MasterWord Services, Inc. Each spent countless hours working to ensure that the English text remains true to the original text and teachings and expresses key concepts and terminologies both clearly and consistently.

Ludmila and Alexandre Golovine have provided generous support, tireless effort and enthusiasm for *The Origin Is Pure* as well as for its predecessor, *Just Use This Mind*. These books would not exist in the English translation without their whole hearted commitment to every aspect of this project.

At Bright Sky Press, Lucy Chambers and Cristina Adams edited the manuscript to present the essence of the message in accessible language to the general public. Ellen Cregan brought her artistic touch to the layout and feel of the book.

Special thanks go to Jui-min Su, Jung-Wei Chen, Olga Daggs, Jennifer Farmer and Adrianne Poyet-Smith for their many helpful suggestions throughout the project and for their diligence in reviewing the manuscript. Larry Payne, Ludmila and Alexandre Golovine, Eric Sun, Heng-Yin Yang, Naishin Chang and many others offered invaluable suggestions during the editorial process.

Finally, thank you to my brother, Dr. Tien-Sheng Hsu, for his support in publishing the Chinese version of this book in Taiwan.

Shih, Miao Tsan

TABLE OF CONTENTS

PREFACE:
FIND THE DIVINE WITHIN

Emerges through the departed branch, fragrance of flowers

Surfaces from the playful moon, shadow of past memories

Losing the Essence to the Invasion of the Five Barbarians

Rooted is Emperor Kuangyin's governing in the hearts

of the Six Patriarchs.

The cultural, moral and religious notions of various countries and regions once served as standards for human ideology and conduct. Those traditional social structures and systems guided and confined people's thoughts. People spent their lives in pursuit of a stated purpose and ideals, and societies around the world were able to achieve relative stability through the use of such cultural structures. Since the beginning of the Industrial Revolution, people of the respective cultures have had an increasing desire to pursue the pleasures of a materialistic life. This desire in the collective mentality has promoted the rapid development of science and technology, as modern civilization has glorified the value of science to explore, pursue and create an abundance of physical phenomena. However, as we have cultivated the so-called spirit of science, we have fragmented the wholeness of life. This fragmentation conditions the individual to seek truth outside the Mind.

As mankind transitions from traditional cultural systems to a modern civilization centered on technology, life's focus shifts from spiritual and moral nourishment to the pursuit of—and the dependency on—materialism. Thus the emphasis on external phenomena in order to obtain sensory pleasures, and our reliance on these stimulations becomes overwhelming. People caught in this cycle depend upon the development of more and more phenomena. Such a vicious cycle increases the desire to seek the truth outside the Mind. Life therefore diverges from the central truth of existence, just as arrows disperse from a strong crossbow. The pressure is too powerful to be restrained or reversed.

Modern man's approach to the physical world and the way events occur is to analyze and pursue phenomena, then grasp and become dependent upon what has been discovered. This approach robs mankind of the ability to comprehend the true principle of the formation and transformation of phenomena. People caught up in the pursuit of phenomena lose their infinite, innate creative force. They surrender this power to the environment and develop their internal experiences and ideas through interactions with the world around them. Tremendous changes in lifestyle and the predominance of a technology-centric duality, which advocates seeking the truth externally without enlightening the mind, prove to be very powerful distractions.

As a result, mankind is rapidly losing sight of what is valuable in the political, economic, cultural, religious and moral systems of the past. These systems break down with such speed because nothing meaningful seems to emerge from them. People, sensing the inability to generate meaning, lose respect for the old traditions. Without such structures, however, people feel such a sense of instability that they collectively manifest a variety of calamities in the world.

The advancement of Internet technology, the rapid flow of information, and the popularization of concepts such as globalization and the global village further accelerate the breakdown of regional and isolationistic cultural, religious and moral systems. The background of modern life is different from the world in which the older means of existence flourished. Just as it is difficult to sow the same seeds in different types of soils, modern man is unable to accept and believe in the culture, moral values and meaning of the life that once prevailed. At the same time, citizens of the modern world have lost the ability to find meaning and purpose for their existence.

If you ask an atheist, "Where will people go after death?" he will probably respond, "I do not know." If you ask someone from modern society, "What is the purpose of life?" it is unlikely she would say the purpose is to become a sage or to perfect virtues such as altruism, reciprocity, cordiality, wisdom and honesty. Modern society emphasizes individuality and diversity. Without an awareness regarding the purpose, basis and possibility of the practice of diversity, the concept of individuality that emerges is ego-driven. Despite any diversity, it will be scattered and short of standards. This disorderly plurality further confuses people, and consequently the rootless individuality that ensues will have no positive impact.

The civilizations established over the course of human history have generally been established on duality, in which people have sought the truth outside the Mind. The isolated, regional and traditional social cultures that have existed for the past two thousand years are divergent, but those traditional societies, due to their isolation and regional characteristics, were all relatively stable. Now these two conditions no longer exist, and it is difficult to maintain the relative stability these societies once had.

We now find ourselves in a transition between the traditional social culture and the futuristic modern culture. We live in a society that is ever-changing and unstable, undergoing constant proliferation and diversification. We can call this a Bardo culture—or a transitional culture—in which rapid changes in living conditions create a gap between the traditional culture and the modern one. Unstable minds created by the gap lead to unstable phenomena, which in turn manifest various natural disasters, wars and social upheavals. Such disasters and social problems cause people to lose faith in the stability of the materialistic world on which they so heavily depend.

People, and indeed all sentient beings, are trying to find a way to the ultimate liberation and happiness. The desire is to achieve stability again. Because the ideologies of the modern world are incompatible with the traditional ways of life, modern man lacks the means to return to a traditional social structure. Thus it is perceived that the traditional systems no longer satisfy the needs of modern life, but people seek freedom from the constraints of traditional systems and establish a unified way of life that breaks away from the existing social framework.

The new system is a work-in-progress, but the breakdown of traditional cultural, moral and religious systems is approaching ever faster. Social deconstruction and reconstruction confuse modern people, and as a result they feel lost. Further clouding the situation is the fact that the system created in order to break through the existing social framework is framed in another structure, which people fail to recognize as having the same fundamental nature of the old system. In such a belief system, ego becomes the true God—or the true Buddha—whether the believer, past or present, is religious or not.

Ideology based on ego becomes a sacred temple that cannot be profaned. As modern people reject the traditional faith-centric system, they are entrapped within another system built by the same self-centric egos. With their ego attachment they perceive reality in terms of "inner" and "outer," creating various problems for themselves. Modern man's attempt to find liberation through any new system will ultimately fail if that system is based on dualistic attachment. Just like the attempt to capture the moon on the water, the pursuit of liberation will be a waste of effort.

Order and stability will not be achieved for the new era by leading the world into another dualistic system. Only by inwardly breaking through the ego can we truly discover the universal law of formation and transformation that should be the basis of a stable new culture. This law transcends space, time and structure. It is a principle without regional prejudice or limitation. A new era based on this principle allows for a convergent civilization that is open, diverse and based on Mind-centric unity.

This civilization promotes the universal truth, which subdues the dualistic belief that advocates the search for truth externally. Many religions in the course of history have been founded in order to teach the universal truth. Unfortunately, after the formation of such belief systems people became lost in the historical aspect, cultural details and bureaucracy of the respective religious structures, despite the original mission of propagating the truth. They mistook the structure, the system or its historical background as the purpose of religion. This perception only obscures the real truth, which must ultimately be conveyed.

The universal truth is the law of creation under which life is formed, and each of us has the innate ability to create his or her own life phenomena. Regardless of the source of that creative force, whether it comes from God or is innate to human beings, each of us can create our own ideas, thoughts, personality, appearance, environment, relationships and diseases. According to our own creative force, which is shaped according to our ego attachment, we create all kinds of phenomena and form our egocentric universe. We always live in a world generated by our own creative force.

The innate creative force has limitless, multidirectional potential. These phenomena, which are boundless, originate from the innate creative force and the underlying Law of Creation. In other words, all phenomena can be traced to a single source of creativity and an operating principle, which is that none of us can separate himself from this innate creative force and its law of formation. Neither can anyone step outside the world she has created. To solve our problems we must focus on the creative force itself instead of what it has already created. We must re-create in accordance with our creative force and its corresponding principle.

The purpose of promoting the universal truth is not to convert everyone to Buddhism, nor is it to abandon religion and traditional social systems. The purpose is to find a revitalizing, civilized manner of expression for religions, traditional societies and the next generation. With the universal truth as the focus, people who spread religious doctrines may stay true to the original purpose of their religious teaching, while those who care about humanity may return to the root of today's problems and resolve any of various issues through collective, unified effort.

It is my hope that believers in traditional religions, cultures and morals, as well as non-believers, can understand the universal truth and live accordingly. It is through this manner of living that order can be re-established in the new era. The order of this new era will be multidirectional, open, stable, peaceful, unified and convergent. It is history's most challenging task to create this new way of living, but it is also the only appropriate means of addressing the predicament of humanity, now and in the future.

I have assembled in the following pages some of the content from the lectures I have given throughout the United States. This content explores the truth of living in accordance with the nature of the Mind in a way that can be grasped with relative ease. As you ponder its content, not only will misunderstandings you may have about Buddhist teaching be clarified but you will also learn to embrace the universal truth in your life. As a result, your spirituality will be elevated.

This mountain monk wrote Just Use This Mind, *and a few people responded. Now* The Origin Is Pure *makes its debut, like the yellowish-green leaves in the mountains. Miao Tsan has a message, but words are not adequate to convey it.*

He climbed the mountain ridge and escaped to Da-Yu. In the distraction of the thin wind and slanting rain, he had one shot at discovering the emptiness of the self among the hunters. One monk speaks, another moves. The wind and flag are both beside the point that is the Mind. Now, as it always has been, Caoxi Spring is channeled toward the five lakes. It seems foolish to merely point out the truth here and there. Now that this book is at last in readers' hands, what else remains to be preached? For the masses that will smell the impure odor of this paper, how can the true fragrance of Dharma be expressed?

Words may fail, but the power to speak remains.
Listen to the verse that shakes the heavens and earth:

Buddha never named himself Sakyamuni.
In my home pond the lotus roots were planted.
Ask me from what refuge I came,
I will say without hesitation that I am from the Five Platforms.

Five Platform Spirits, the dance platform spirit.
Unsettled and wandering in the unfulfilled midnight dream.
Quietly and attentively, there is spring in every step.

Please allow me to leave with you this other poem:

The strong wind swirls up dust, blocking the clear sky.
Even the sound of the bell at the temple can be annoying.
Where the butterflies and the fragrance of flowers overflow
Never has a single petal fallen to the mundane world.

Shih, Miao Tsan

Vairocana Zen Monastery, California, USA

1 AN OPPORTUNITY TO TRANSFORM LIFE

Movement creates shadows;

In quiet the dark mountain spirit comes alive.

One wise word from the Buddha,

Living utterance that turns stones into gold.

Reverence for the Truth Is the Only Wise Form of Reverence

The point of spiritual practice is to illuminate the Mind; hence, the Buddha Dharma comes from searching with a reverent mind. Therefore, reverence is learning with a humble mind. It is not the deliberate, superficial respect that is rooted in prejudices based on inferiority or superiority. Instead, learning results from the desire to seek, improve and gain a deeper understanding of the truth. If we cannot relinquish our attachments, we will have difficulty realizing any changes in our lives. Attachments naturally make people think that their vision, thoughts and behavior—and ultimately everything they do—is right. Once the idea of "right" is established, exclusivity is established as well. Others may speak the truth, but the person who thinks his or her way of seeing is "right" may not listen. It is impossible to learn when the mind is not empty.

Learning is restricted if one does so with mental rigidity. With an inflexible mind, even if we are aware of the truth, its application to life remains a challenge. Buddha is the Primordial Mind. The

Mind can give rise to immeasurable, boundless manifestation. Our appearance, thoughts, social relationships and lifestyle are all reflections of the karma within the Mind and our personal characteristics, or our attachments. When we find it difficult to change our physical appearance or to leave the surrounding environment and interpersonal relationships, it indicates that the Mind is functioning within a restricted range. Even if it is stable, its vitality is relatively low. If the Mind is free, flexible and unrestricted, it can create new realities.

Most people have a strong sense of ego. They constantly interact with the subjective relationships and external environments their egos have created, and their reality is bound by circumstances that cannot be eliminated. If life is not smooth, the mind suffers pain. However, with awareness that is vitally alive we can be flexible enough to accept, improve and even transform our own environment and relationships. Thus we become free in all circumstances, whether adverse or favorable. In the latter, we not only know the reason and result of our prosperity but can also create more favorable circumstances for the prosperity to come. In adversity we are able to recognize the problem and its root cause. Therefore, we can handle problems calmly and transform predicaments into opportunities for growth.

We must be reverent in order to make the awareness vitally alive and know the truth. In other words, we must open our minds. Only with an open mind can anyone learn and grow more freely. Many people are very respectful to others, but only under certain circumstances. For example, due to a bureaucratic hierarchy they may be respectful to their supervisors at work. This kind of respect does not necessarily originate within the heart. Therefore, true reverence is required so that we can know the wisdom in Buddha Dharma. What Buddha taught is worth learning. The principles are true without exception, and they can improve our lives. Any reverence we show should be based on that recognition.

A lively awareness means letting go of attachments. Reverence to the truth is the true, wise reverence. It is not about being reverent because we have to be or are forced to be so. One might be reverent toward his master or at the temple, but once he leaves the temple and the master a completely different person emerges. That individual is no longer as kind and respectful to others as before. This is merely superficial respect. It demonstrates that the reverence is a result of the inner restrictions of a mind's attachments. This kind of mind does not possess flexibility. It cannot truly learn, nor can it free itself of stereotypes. To a certain extent, this type of respect for others is only a temporary suppression of the ego.

Reverence first requires an understanding that "all sentient beings have the Buddha Nature." We should recognize and respect the Buddha Nature, Self-Nature—the innate creative force that each of us possesses—whether we perceive it as good or evil. Those you despise may become affluent in the future. Take the story of Emperor Kuangyin Zhao, from ancient Chinese history: Zhao had once been very poor and disrespected, but eventually he became the founding emperor of the Song Dynasty. The mind's growth has unlimited potential, the manifestations of which can differ in myriad ways. We need to respect the fact that each person has the Primordial Mind, which in turn has a limitless ability to create. Therefore, anyone—

everyone—has the potential to change and improve. Some people would criticize a vegetarian who once ate meat for not having virtuous roots, but virtuous roots are acquired through cultivation. Because each of us has a unique set of life circumstances and accordingly a separate path to follow, we each go through the process of spiritual cultivation and growth in our own way and at our own pace.

Various phenomena will appear as the Mind functions in its different ways. Phenomena, however, are not eternal. Your appearance in this life is not the same as your appearance in the previous life or in the life to come. The destitution you might suffer today does not indicate that there will be poverty tomorrow, nor do one's current fame and riches foretell a bright future. Due to the Mind's ability to function in different directions, sentient beings possess different karmic causes and conditions that manifest as various personalities, appearances and environments. Criminals are able to engage in criminal activities because the Mind also has that potential. The Mind's ability to create is miraculous.

We must put this creative ability to good use because it can lead us to heaven or to hell. Indeed, the desire to learn and to employ our creative ability is what leads us to a reverent state of mind. When we see others' prosperity, the respect we might show for their professional success or good relationships is beside the point. What we should take from their example is the realization that the Mind has enormous potential to change. It is through changed thoughts that such incredible positive creation in life can take place.

Why is it that the Buddha's disciples could become sages and obtain Buddhahood within only a lifetime's practice but modern practitioners progress so slowly? Why is it that some people can improve once they put effort into their practice while, for others, the challenge to improve their lives continues even after years of practice? This may indicate that the Mind's ability to create is headed in the wrong direction; that it lacks strength in its application or is guided by misunderstanding. Ordinary people can become emperors, while the rich may become destitute. It all depends on the direction and extent to which one applies the Mind.

The Mind possesses an infinite potential to create change. The Mind has the power to create a better world. The key is the way we should use the Mind to improve and enhance our life. A great deal of suffering can result from the lack of awareness as to how one should use the Mind.

The phenomena created by the Mind can change. Just as facial expressions change constantly, the manifestations of the Mind are ever-changing. The form of our thoughts, bodies and relationships disappears immediately after the appearance, just as the energy state of cells in the body can be transformed immediately after synthesis. Wisdom lies in how we live with this inevitable nature of life. The simultaneity of phenomenal appearance and disappearance is a universal law from which no one can be exempt. Therefore, we must live in harmony with that principle. Suffering will be brought forth by any thought or act that is not in harmony with this law.

We human beings have many of our own ideas, and the attachments deeply rooted in our minds are difficult to change. If a person attempts to use these rigid personalities, thoughts and inner attachments to deal with the constantly changing momentary phenomena in the universe, he or she will naturally face hardships. Whether or not one has a spiritual practice, neither spiritual nor worldly affairs will succeed if one deviates from the universal principles. Ego can be broken and changed, but the universal principles cannot be violated. The Buddha was someone who fully understood these universal laws; he lived and practiced them until at last he achieved the ultimate wholeness of life.

The Creative Force of Life Is Neither Holy Nor Mundane

To be convinced of a principle, we must decide whether it is universal and free of exception. Take, for example the idea of God creating man. God in the Catholic Church is neither that of Protestant Christianity nor that of Islam; Buddhism does not acknowledge the concept of God, and atheists have no belief in God at all. Therefore, the idea of God creating man lacks universality.

Is the Buddhist teaching that all beings have Buddha Nature universally true? This question gives rise to another: Among the global population of seven billion, only two hundred million are Buddhists. Consequently, is it valid for Buddhists to believe that all beings have Buddha nature?

If you are a Buddhist, you might take this teaching for granted simply because you have heard it for so long. However, you must know the truth of this idea. Otherwise, what you believe will simply be groundless superstition. You have been taught to have faith in it without understanding what Buddha Nature truly is.

It is natural to inherit what we have been taught, be it Confucianism, Daoism or Christianity. Therefore, unless one clearly understands the true meaning of Buddhist teaching, a Buddhist is no different from another religious person who believes only in her own school of thought. Each person not only has the ability to believe in an idea but also has the ability to act according to that idea, shaping himself to fit the mold of the idea and living with that new self. If the Christian God reflects this principle and process, then He *is* universal. This is also true of the Buddha Nature. The point is whether the idea exists as a principle or as a specific phenomenon. From the Buddhist perspective, it is possible to achieve eternity without necessarily believing in God; in other words, the concepts of Buddha Nature and God both have innate existence, and each exists as a "thing-in-itself."

Every religion or philosophy acknowledges that man possesses a creative life force. In the West, this creativity originates in God; in Buddhism, it originates in Buddha Nature; in Zen Buddhism, it is called the Mind. The term "Mind" in Zen Buddhism is a comprehensive one used to simultaneously describe the source of this creative force, the function of this creative force and the result of its function.

The Mind has always been. It is formless and shapeless, but it is also omnipresent. No one can exist apart from the essence of this Mind and its principle of phenomena manifestation. This idea exists in Western religions as well. The statement, "God is the Creator of all," means God is in each and every one of us. The occidental God, too, is eternal and omnipresent. The Western approach toward the propagation of that concept lends itself to an anthropomorphic representation of God, whereby God is perceived as a specific being who created all. This approach has led to the materialization and deification of the idea of God.

This principle of creativity is not a deified God-being; instead, it transcends the distinctions of mundane versus sacred or of superiority versus inferiority. There is a Zen Buddhist saying, "*Dao* is in pee and poo." *Dao* here is the universal principle that takes on various appearances. Zen Buddhism says *Dao* is even in every secretion, but few Westerners would say the same of God. Their God is believed to be holy, and holy is understood by discriminating between that which is exalted and that which is considered low. On the contrary, Buddha Nature as a principle acknowledges no such distinction but instead exists in every person and thing. Thus we have the saying, "*Dao* is in pee and poo."

Once there was a Zen master who awoke in the middle of the night to the call of nature. In traditional Buddhist prayer halls, the statue of the Buddha was located in the center of the hall, and the monks would sleep along the sides of the space. The outhouse was outside, far away, so the master began to urinate right in the hall. Another master rose to stop him, asking how he could urinate in the presence of the Buddha. He replied, "If you could tell me of a place free of the Buddha's presence, I would go there," by which he meant that the Buddha is everywhere. This is also true of the Mind. There is no place free of the Mind.

Buddha Nature, or the Mind, is not holy. It is simply the creative force that each person possesses. For instance, if you were to hear me preach these concepts, the fact that you could hear and feel while listening to my words would prove that you have the ability to perceive. The ability to hear is universal, but your attachment guides you to listen for the particulars; to interpret my preaching, judge whether you like or dislike; to agree or disagree with what you hear; and eventually to live out those beliefs.

It is the same as you read the words of this book. The question if what you choose to notice or interpret is right or wrong is a separate issue. To talk about the purpose and uplifting of your life, you must understand the universal truth. It is through this understanding that the secret of existence and formation of life can be found. Only after discovering this secret can any of us solve the problems of life.

Change Comes from Changing Your Mind

The past, present and future represent time. The vast variety of personalities in the world represents different directions that the function of the Mind takes, in turn constituting spatial change. A universal principle—but only a universal principle—is not limited by time and space. Furthermore, each person has a mind that functions in different directions and brings about different consequences with which he or she has to live. In the past, you created your old self based on your belief. In this present, moment you create your current self based on your current belief, and you will do the same with respect to your future self.

The Mind has neither shape nor form, but it is everywhere and creates all. God is the same. Therefore, the Mind is God. Both are creators. This Creator's functioning principle is "true emptiness, transcendental existence," meaning that the Mind gives rise to the appearance of phenomena in this very moment and yet this very instance of existence is itself disappearance. No sooner does the

Mind reflect an appearance than the very appearance disappears. The moment you hear a sound, it disappears; no one can keep a sound nor identify the actual hearer of the sound.

It is the function of the Mind that enables you to hear. People commonly believe we hear through the coordination of the ears and the brain, but in fact hearing is not based on either. The Mind, by nature, is capable of hearing; it is an innate ability, shapeless and formless. However, the ordinary being, given his strong attachments, is no longer capable of hearing sound outside the conduit defined by his attachments. For human beings, the strong tendency to seek sound outside the Mind results in the physical manifestations of the auditory organ and the brain, including all the mutually dependent physiological structures that enable hearing. However, in reality it is the Mind that hears. When someone is very focused on doing something, he or she cannot hear you no matter what you say; whether a person hears or not depends on whether the Mind is at work.

A sound that is heard indicates the Mind's transcendental existence, and the simultaneous disappearance of the sound represents the Mind's nature of emptiness. Thus the Mind is concurrently emptiness and transcendental existence. This is the fundamental truth of Buddhism. Because instantaneous existence means disappearance, what you pursue is beyond pursuit. When the formless Mind, or the Creator, projects appearances it requires the synergy of various conditions. Therefore, the idea of transcendental existence is based on the Buddhist concept called dependent-arising.

Body cells are amalgamations, as are the environment, society, human relationships and all other perceivable phenomena. The interrelatedness of phenomena means that one particular appearance must be connected to all other related appearances and, taken together, they reflect the synthesized appearance of an indivisible whole. Dependent-arising is nothing more than the coming together of causes and conditions. Through the synthesis of causes and conditions phenomena arise.

Even when it comes to defining our "self," we cannot identify any "point" within the totality of dependent-arising appearance—manifested by the Mind—as an independently existing "I." This inability to separate ourselves from the whole of reality is much like how the body is composed of many cells, not a single one of which can represent the self. The true "I" is the formless Mind. It creates appearances according to its principle, but in no single appearance does it materialize as the Creator. Dependent-arising changes moment by moment, and consequently phenomena are impermanent. However, neither the concept of dependent-arising nor that of impermanence fully explains the origin of life, which is of course the Mind.

Impermanence describes the limitless, ever-changing creative power of the Mind. It is comprised of a series of instantaneous existences created by the Mind. It is the Mind that gives you emotions, thoughts and perceptions, which in turn cause real changes in your life. Therefore, the Mind is the true master of life. Now, if a body or a thought vanishes the instant it comes into being, how can a person be considered alive? To illustrate this from a medical perspective, it is the presence of brain waves that indicates life and its functions, which produce thoughts, emotions and perceptions.

One thought after another appears in your mind, and the

ability to create these ever-changing thoughts makes you alive, even though no single thought is alive. Thought is a kind of energy, which, according to physics, cannot create itself but must be created. When your emotions change from high to low and your thoughts vary from this to that, it is in this stream of emotions and feelings that you are alive, even though these emotions and thoughts are not alive.

Brain waves are a kind of energy or a material phenomena. The Mind as the origin of life (the Creator) can cause materials and energy to change. In order to change life and phenomena, we must find and rely on this Creator to create and to change instead of seeking answers from the phenomena. When people cannot eliminate pain, worry and moods, it is because they have not found the Creator, meaning that which really makes us alive. When we are unable to align ourselves with the Creator, we will not be able to create significant changes in our lives, regardless of how hard we might try.

Everything you currently are is the result of the Creator's work. Thus we have a question: Because everything comes from your mind, why do others matter? If someone causes your frustrations, then he becomes your Creator; you might as well worship him. When you habitually depend on people or things in your life in order to determine how to feel, your mind creates emotions in accordance with that dependence. The truth is that all feelings can only come from within you. Here is an example I often use to illustrate the point: If you are in a bad mood and cannot eliminate your erroneous thinking, what good does it do to have ten masseuses working on you?

The process of changing your relationships or surroundings is similar to changing a thought to a laugh or a thought to a cry. No matter how many people are around you, regardless of how strong their influences might be, if your mind does not give rise to a single thought of laughter you will not laugh. People often relinquish their ownership of the ability to laugh or cry, instead becoming dependent on "external conditions," which, in Buddhist terminology, refers to the "search for truth outside the Mind." However, what is not yours is by definition beyond your reach and grasp. To change relationships and all the other conditions of your life, you must elevate your true self. Whenever you feel stranded by your external environment, in reality you are trapped by your internal thoughts. All situations and their problems are the result of how your mind and character function. Thus it is the framework of your mind's functioning that must be changed.

Given that the thought to cry or be angry dissolves as soon as it enters your mind, how can you change it? One way is to decide to laugh. While the thought to cry vanishes the instant it arises, the reason we keep crying is because the mind keeps creating the same thought through the same channel, perpetuating the impulse to cry. Various predicaments that people encounter in life are similar to a thought to cry entering the mind. Similarly, the way to put an end to these predicaments is to put an end to the thoughts, if you can manage to do so. You must understand this point in order to turn away from the situation already created and turn to the Creator for change. Therefore, you must be careful not to mistake consequence for cause.

Your thoughts, character, body, environment and relationships, whether good or bad, are results created by your mind. The people who dislike you or are mean to you: who created them? Without you, none of them would exist the way they do. Do not believe there is another world outside the Mind—a world as you see it. Instead, practice the teaching that "there is no truth outside the Mind." Right now, your mind is reflecting the relationships it creates. If these relationships are not desirable, you must begin to function from a different mental framework in order to achieve a different result.

The observance of imperfections in others is, from the Buddhist perspective, a reflection of the imperfections in yourself. If you feel strange about a person standing in front of you, it is like looking into a mirror and seeing a strange reflection, since that person standing in front of you is really a reflection of your own mind. People will appear the way your mind projects them to be, so there is no need to act surprised with the relationships you have. The Mind is like a big mirror that reflects all the appearances you have created, including your thoughts, body, surroundings and relationships. To put it simply, as you sit contemplating my words you have a certain perspective on me, the person next to you, the furniture and the outside world. However, when you turn your head those perspectives change. Similarly, when the Mind works in a different way, relationships change. Now, imagine you dislike the person sitting to your right, so you push him. If your relationships with all the others remain the same, how much can your relationship with the person on the right really change? A person acts as his attachment guides him to act, but this kind of action does little to substantively change his or her relationships. Only when he or she can voluntarily change how the mind functions can everything change.

Your current relationships with the people around you, as well as with all the furnishings of your life, are one indivisible whole created by your mind. If your attachments or habits cause you to see the person next to you as unpleasant, and you try to change your entire relationship by pushing that person, your hand and the person are but a small part of the whole. This kind of action—which is conditionally dependent, isolated to an individual or object—does little to bring about overall change. Unfortunately, this is exactly what people commonly try to do when they want to change their reality.

If your mind continues to work the same way and does the same things, no problem can be resolved. To resolve problems with your attachments and habits, you must understand that it is a dualistic concept based on the process of discriminating between the internal and the external, or the subject and the object. People do not realize that all the relationships they encounter and see actually make up one indivisible whole. You cannot simply dissect the whole into pieces and then try to change one particular relationship. To believe others have caused your problems in the first place and then to try to isolate those problems from the whole can never bring about genuine change. However, the instant you change how your mind works, every relationship changes.

The universe is constantly changing, but humans, directed by their attachments, keep themselves busy within certain confines. Their efforts produce no progress. The Mind, however, is a whole. No appearance can exist outside the one and only Creator. How can there be creations that can be dissected? If you could be separated from the appearances in your life, there would be two creations—a body created by you and the appearances created by life—but that is not the case.

Each person has a mind that works according to its own principles. Problems only occur when the individual's mind creates relationships that he or she alone will experience through the mold shaped by his or her character and personality. Your inner attachment and character determine the kinds of phenomena and relationships you encounter, hence the saying, "A person's character is his fate."

Each of us creates her own way of thinking, as well as her own character. These come to epitomize our surroundings and relationships. As our circumstances reflect our inner thinking, the problems with those circumstances are, in fact, the problems of our inner character. According to Buddhism, your karma—your environment and relationships, whether good or bad—is brought forth by your mind. Imagine many ropes in your mind, weaving together your relationships and other circumstances—manifestations or appearances—and each rope connects your mind to one particular person or circumstance. To gain freedom from a particular situation, you must first find the rope tied to it and then release it.

No external appearance or circumstance can exist unless such a thought happens within the mind. For example, we must know which thought to release in order to be free of the situation or free of a particular person or problem. Without loosening the inner hook, no matter how hard we try to push the problem away, it will come back again. Thus the problem is only momentarily solved. Instead, we must first acknowledge that we cause all our problems. Only then can we determine what thought causes which problem and figure out how to let go. This process requires practice.

A joyful mind glows with beautiful spring blossoms;

An angry mind burns out winter mountain chrysanthemums;

A sorrowful mind falls low from its great height

like a summer waterfall;

A happy mind shines an autumn moon over the dike.

2 BASIC PRINCIPLES OF ZEN STUDIES

The Sixth Patriarch revealed the fountain of Truth.

Master Da Zhu brings out the essence of the inner pearl.

Master Da An crosses the river of suffering to reveal
the purity within.

Master Da Hui guides all beings onto the true path.

Samsara: When Life Is Tied Down by Attachments

According to Buddha, there are 84,000 methods of spiritual cultivation. However, each of us must determine his actual goal in cultivation, according to the true meaning of the statement that "everyone possesses his or her own Buddha Nature." The purpose of spiritual cultivation is to discover and use your own Buddha Nature, the Primordial Mind. Buddha said upon his enlightenment, "How incredible! How incredible! All living creatures possess Buddha's wisdom and virtue, but due to their erroneous thinking this wisdom and virtue cannot be fulfilled." Thus the main point of religious inquiry is to dissolve the erroneous thinking and attachment within the mind.

Erroneous thinking, by twisting reality and polluting the mind, creates obstacles in life. It is the root of the suffering that occurs between life and death. There is an old saying: "Each mind is as different as each face." Different minds create different karmas, in turn bringing forth different bodies, families and careers. Therefore, when you blame your frustrations on the external environment it simply indicates that you do not know such frustration is the result of not knowing how to face the karma you have created. Because the mind habitually creates the worries in your life, practice is needed in order to turn a worry-making mind into one that is free of worry.

Thus goes the ancient saying, "There is no cultivation other than to recognize the source; and once the source is identified both life and death can be put to rest." Cultivation should start from the proper perspective: Your vexations come from the mind, so they should be eliminated from the mind. It is a very straightforward concept. There is no worry unless the Mind generates it. Due to the different paths the Mind can take, personality, culture, background and abilities will vary from one person to another. Consequently, there are many methods and belief systems that can help people free themselves from their particular situations and move toward their innate nature. Such methods and belief systems can help them recognize the root of life and fulfill the creativity of their otherwise confused minds. Regardless of one's religious tradition, it is essential to recognize that "All is the Mind."

People, due to their different karmas, live in various places and have distinct appearances. Similarly, within Buddhism even the various sects have resulted from different karmas created by different minds. Your mind creates your unique situation and stance in life. You begin in a state of ignorance where you do not realize that you will create your own life. Subsequently, you try to become aware of the life-creating Mind, and then you begin to employ the Mind's creative power consciously in order to move toward perfection. Your current karma is the only raw material the formless Mind can use to transform your life. Naturally, one person's method of realizing the mind's essence will be different from that of another, but that does not mean one is necessarily better. That would be like saying a hammer is the best tool simply because you are used to it.

Tools are used to do work, and methods are applied toward the achievement of goals. All concepts and methods of spiritual cultivation exist for the purpose of eradicating attachment from the mind. So, unless we are guided by this understanding it is very easy for our cultivation to deviate from the truth. People tend to have arguments about which spiritual method is best. For instance, within Buddhism some people claim that Theravada Buddhism is the best because it maintains the fundamentals of Buddhism. Others, however, claim that the esoteric teaching of Vajrayana is superior because it is the fastest, most effective method. Still others favor Zen Buddhism or Pure Land Buddhism. These kinds of arguments are no better than workers arguing that the hammer, the saw, the screwdriver or the shovel is the best tool.

Language is a tool, as well. You speak English when in America and Chinese when in Taiwan or Mainland China. One cannot fairly state that Chinese is better than English. It is natural that people have different opinions and use different methods due to their different karmas and situations, but the common purpose of all spiritual practices is to help people free themselves from erroneous beliefs. Therefore, you should make use of such tools as Pure Land, Zen, Theravada, the esoteric teachings or other spiritual practices to correct erroneous thoughts, eliminate deep-rooted attachments, recognize the Mind and create a perfect life of clarity and purity. As the old saying goes, "There is no new method other than to recover one's original nature." Basically, to cultivate your thinking is basically to recover your innate nature but not to create a new one.

People generally cannot accept the idea that their thoughts are erroneous. Buddha said that if everyone thinks he is right then there is no such thing as a universal truth. If your belief is only applicable under certain circumstances, it is not truth. It was the belief of the ancient saints that different karmas would result in different situations, whereby the individual would become trapped in the prison of grasping illusions. Thus we have the statement, "If you search for your Buddha Nature from dawn to dusk, it is within a single thought." Some people, even as they acknowledge the different karmas and the different methods and degrees of cultivation we each need, might feel compelled to say, "It is not fair." Actually, everything is fair: It is fair that each mind can function. It is also fair that the different ways of the Mind bring forth different appearances and karmas with which one has to live.

Accordingly, the Mind's function brings forth appearance. When you meditate with a mind that is clear and calm, you may experience the inner perception of a radiant light. That light is the pure appearance of the Mind. However, if you meditate with the intention of seeing the light, there will be no such light. The desire to see the light is an attachment to phenomena, and it causes the mind to work differently.

This is how an uncultivated mind works: The mind functions and accordingly manifests a certain appearance. When a person perceives that appearance, he then holds onto it; and in response the mind acts out a second function, which brings forth a second appearance and so on. From birth to present to future, this is how people allow their minds to continuously attach to various appearances. "Seeking the truth outside the Mind" fetters the Mind by suppressing its creativity and replacing its proactive nature with reaction, thereby creating "the prison of grasping illusion."

People allow their minds to become attached to one appearance after another. When there is a change in the appearance currently being grasped, they grasp the changed appearance yet again. In this way, people create a life of *samsara*, or transmigration. As the individual's mind changes with the flow of appearances and thoughts, her life is filled with highs and lows. A thought leads to an appearance, which in turn leads to a pursuit that creates another appearance, much like a river flowing downward with one ripple following another. In this way, a life of turbulence is created.

Freedom Is Not to Be Trapped by Appearances

The true nature of the Mind is recognized upon enlightenment, and accordingly it generates thoughts that are not conditioned responses to the external environment. In Buddhism, this stage is referred to as freedom; it is freedom from attachment and the self-created appearances of life. This freedom of body and mind is present in hard times and good times. In life, it is reflected in the way everything manifests.

Spiritual cultivation should start with taming thoughts, so be aware of every thought. Only a mind independent from its thoughts can lead to a body at ease with the karma it has created. Before reaching Nirvana, Master Hui Neng, the Sixth Patriarch of Zen Buddhism, told his disciples that he was about to leave and then answered each of their questions. That very night, after preaching, he meditated until midnight. Then, he suddenly said, "I'm gone," and, indeed, at that instant he achieved Nirvana. With a single thought to leave the body, he did so. His body, with neither treatment nor preservation, has kept well from the Tang Dynasty until now, over a span of 1,400 years. Only a free mind can live a free life and die a free death.

Master Zi Bo, of the Ming Dynasty, also achieved Nirvana through excellent cultivation. He attained enlightenment by focusing his penetrating insight upon the Tang scholar Zhang Zhuo's verse of enlightenment. Zhang Zhuo went to pay his respects to Master Chan Yue, who instead directed him to see Master Shi Shuang. At the first sight of Zhang Zhuo, Master Shi Shuang asked for his surname. He replied, "My surname is Zhang, first name Zhuo." The word *zhuo* means "the clumsy." The Master said, "Even the skillful is beyond pursuit; where do you find the clumsy?" Upon hearing this, Zhang Zhuo was immediately enlightened and uttered the following verse:

> *The Light peacefully shines on all realms innumerable*
> *as the river sands;*
> *The mundane and the sacred are originally all in my family.*
> *Without a single thought, the whole of essence appears;*
> *Just when the six senses stir, it is instantly concealed by clouds.*
> *I tried to eradicate illusions only to gain more trouble;*

To seek after truth is also a deviation.

Follow one's fate without hindrance;

Nirvana, like birth and death, is an illusory appearance.

Why did Master Shi Shuang say, "Even the skillful is beyond pursuit; where do you find the clumsy?" Some people say human nature is innately good, but others say it is innately evil. According to Zen Buddhism, however, the essence of the Mind is neither good nor evil. The quality of good or evil depends on whether good thought or evil thought enters the mind. It is the same with the skillful and the clumsy: Both are functions of the mind, which is of course neither skillful nor clumsy. Through this metaphor, the scholar Zhang Zhuo grasped the concept of the Mind as formless and egoless but nevertheless aware.

It is a trap to identify your mind with its manifestations. Such a trap can only prevent you from recognizing your mind's true nature. You must understand that all dualistic concepts—such as right and wrong, good and evil, true and false—are ways to "seek truth outside the mind." These thoughts seem to be correct simply because your ego is accustomed to them, but they are not by nature correct. An unclear mind is fully dependent on these thoughts for guidance. Contrastingly, the Mind, as the whole universe with limitless light and wisdom, being free of these dualistic beliefs, will instantly illuminate the reality realm in the same way as "the Light peacefully shines on all realms, innumerable as the river sands. The past, present and future are all created by the Mind, as are all appearances.

A Zen master composed a verse upon his enlightenment: "Lift

my hand, I reach the South Star; turn my body around, I lean on the North Star. Sticking my head out, I look above the heavens; who else is just like me?" An enlightened person knows that outside the Mind there is no phenomenon. Naturally, this means the Mind is borderless; even the South Star is within arm's reach, while the North Star is but a jump away. The master's verse is not merely a romantic description of the Mind, because an enlightened mind truly can accommodate the entire void. Another Zen master celebrated his Nirvana with the statement, "My breath is long and smooth, like a ten-thousand-mile wave." In other words, an authentic life in the present moment is everlasting, like the Yangtze River. This is a reality that can be experienced through cultivation. The root of enlightenment is in the Mind, without which one cannot see despite having eyes. The Mind projects its own doings, and therefore, when the Mind is free of erroneous thoughts, it will naturally be filled with all kinds of miracles, peace and wisdom.

One realizes, upon enlightenment, that mountains and rivers and everything are but appearances of the Mind. Most people form a thought-generating habit, which reinforces erroneous beliefs and limits the creativity of the Mind. Lao Tzu once said, "The superior good is like water." In a cup, water is water in the cup; in a bottle, water is water in the bottle; in a creek, water becomes water in the creek. A flexible mind can escape the fetters of controlling habits and be itself. It can give rise to the desired function and refrain from undesired functions, free and at ease in its own karma. When you generate a thought filled with conflict, your mind gets confused, your body feels ill and you end up in a predicament. If your thoughts are beyond your control, so are your relationships, environment, living and, eventually, your life and death. However, when you become the master of your thoughts, your body and life will follow your reign.

The mundane and the sacred are created by the Mind. Thus we have the statement, "The mundane and the sacred are originally all in my family." The Mind is like water: It can either support a boat or topple it. The Mind is a non-duality that transcends the good and the evil, the dualistic concept to which a common mind becomes attached. We must realize that good and evil are but appearances of the Mind. Therefore, in transcending the duality of good and evil to reach the state of neither good nor evil, we recognize that the Mind is the source of all.

"Without a single thought, the entirety of essence appears." In other words, without a thought we are beyond the reach of Buddha or the devil. Each thought has its corresponding manifestation. In the absence of thought, the Mind creates a true, thought-free void. If we can abide in this true void, we can resolve the predicament of life and death. The transmigration between life and death results from the lack of mastery over your thoughts, which endlessly come and go while grasping and pursuing phenomena. To end that cycle, the Mind must function from selfless purity and meld its functioning with the nature of the self. It must do so to the point that every thought originates from the Mind, being inseparable from the source, so that each thought eventually returns to the source.

"Just when the six senses stir, the essence is instantly concealed by clouds." An erroneous belief or attachment cuts up and twists truth through the person's six senses, altering his perceptions to the point that the light of wisdom is concealed and reality cannot be seen. Whatever religion a person may have, most people believe more in themselves than in the religion. They brand everything with their own erroneous thinking and attachments, which distort and conceal truth. Truth never requires our explanation. There is a simple Zen saying: "Clouds are in the sky and water in the vase." Water is always water, and a flower is always a flower. One's explanation and opinion are just that, not the truth itself.

Let us examine the statement, "I tried to eradicate illusions only to gain more trouble." Illusions are not truth; otherwise, it would be impossible to eradicate them. Different karmas result in different predicaments, but no predicament is beyond resolution. For example, if a wandering thought enters your mind during meditation, as long as you remain focused and ignore the thought, it can only disappear. A thought has no essence. One should not guard the void before a thought enters, nor should one follow a thought when it is generated. This way a wandering thought dissolves by itself.

Because our primordial nature has always existed, the point of cultivation is not to create a clean, pure nature but instead to remove any deluded thinking that veils the primordial nature. When you let go of your deep-rooted habits and attachments, truth and light will present themselves to you. Therefore, "I tried to eradicate illusions only to gain more trouble; to seek after truth is also a deviation. Follow one's fate without hindrances; Nirvana, like birth and death, is an illusory appearance."

Master Zi Bo, prior to his enlightenment, heard Zhang Zhuo's verse in a temple. He was very perplexed by the part, "I tried to eradicate illusions only to gain more trouble; to seek after truth is also a deviation." He wondered whether it should be, "I eradicated illusions and there will be no more trouble; I seek truth and leave behind faults." He spent his every moment pondering it, his mind perplexed by the meaning of the verse. All-consumed by the wish to know the answer, his other thoughts were suppressed. But when even that single thought to find the answer was finally broken down, dualistic distinctions were wholly eradicated from his mind and he achieved enlightenment. This story illustrates how one type of Zen practice, such as that of the koans, breaks down a person's habitual thinking and allows him to let go of attachments. It is possible to use the singular thought of doubt to subdue all other thoughts, and then let go of even that final doubt to reveal the Buddha nature.

Zen Buddhism advocates the cultivation of doubt until it congeals into a mass. Accordingly, every thought is the doubt. The method is not about the use of one's discriminating ego to speculate or poke around for an intellectual answer. The assumption that there is a way to solve a koan through reasoning is essentially an erroneous thought that defeats the purpose of this Zen practice. The elder Zhaozhou was once asked this question, "All returns to One, but to where does One return?" Zhaozhou replied, "I had a cotton shirt made in Qing Zhou. It weighed seven catties." This seems to be a completely irrelevant reply to the question, but if you actually see the relevance in his reply, you have achieved enlightenment. Our attachment to beliefs will only lead to erroneous answers; the Master's unique answer, however peculiar it may seem, represents what Zen followers need in order to release the egoistical I-consciousness and reach the root of the Mind.

Master Zi Bo meditated over the verse, concentrating on it to the extent that eating and sleeping lost their appeal and his face became swollen. At his moment of enlightenment, the swelling vanished. During his last years, Master Zi Bo was framed for another's crime and imprisoned. He decided it was time to leave the chaos of this world for his next destination and thereby continue spreading Buddhist teachings. He gave his followers their final instructions, took his bath, sat down and, after a few utterances of "*Vairocana,*" departed for the future world. Cao Zhizhi, one of his disciples at the time and a high-level official, came to the prison to bid farewell to his master. Upon Cao's arrival, Master Zi Bo opened his eyes once more, smiled and bid goodbye to his disciple.

How could a Zen master enjoy the liberty of life and death as he wished? When our mind is its own master, our thoughts, body and even life and death are free. The ultimate suffering in life is a mind enslaved by itself, trapped in undesirable thoughts and appearances, longing hopelessly for the desired outcomes but being unable to manifest as it wishes.

Zen cultivation should start from the Mind, with clean, pure thoughts that usher in a clean, clear world known as the Pure Land. The impure mind cannot manifest the Pure Land, nor will the Pure Land present itself simply because you are practicing certain methods. Chanting scriptures and incantations, or meditating, is simply a method of cultivation. They should not be mistaken for true cultivation itself, which is the release of ego attachment. Any spiritual approach, whether it is Buddhism or another spiritual tradition, aims to calm, purify, illuminate and enlighten the Mind. A mind that has undergone no such cultivation has but an obscure sense of the source and destination, the emergence and disappearance of its thoughts, and its true nature. This is ignorance, because this person does not know what his or her real life is.

If a person cannot create the thoughts he or she desires, all his cultivations will be in vain. In spiritual cultivation, the obstacle is the failure to free the mind of its vexations and attachments. If they cannot be released, it will be impossible to bring forth the Pure Land, enlighten the Mind and be truly free. Without reaching a common understanding that the purification of the mind is absolutely essential, blind faith in your own sect will simply cause disputes—arguments over the legitimacy, effectiveness and significance of various methods of cultivation—without providing an understanding of what methods are truly suited to you. Thus the true purpose of cultivation will remain a mystery.

Freedom Is the Release of Erroneous Beliefs

Any so-called "expedient method" is presented as a shortcut, for the sake of convenience, to those who have no confidence in the teaching. The failure to achieve Nirvana is not a result of not practicing Theravada Buddhism; the failure to become enlightened is not a result of not practicing Zen; the failure to manifest the Pure Land is not a result of not practicing Pure Land Buddhism; and the failure to attain Buddhahood in this lifetime is not a result of not practicing the Esoteric teachings. The desired result of any cultivation method comes about because ordinary people are plagued by attachments and vexations in their minds and are working to free themselves.

The purpose of any Buddhist cultivation is a pure mind, at ease and liberated in every moment and able to manifest reality as it is. To achieve this, one must choose the method by which to eradicate erroneous thinking and ego attachment. Therefore, to assert that a particular method is the legitimate one is to mistake the effect for the cause. It is perfectly reasonable to expect a Pure Land follower to accept the idea of chanting to Amitbha Buddha as a way of reaching the Pure Land, but what really matters is whether he or she is able to manifest the Pure Land from the Mind. If a person's mind is properly prepared with the right causal factors, he or she can certainly reach the Pure Land.

What is the Pure Land? The Mind can manifest all phenomena and function in boundless ways, but as the mind function differs the corresponding karmas and manifestations also differ. Pure Land, defiled land, heaven and hell are all manifestations of the Mind. To reach the desired state requires a corresponding ability of the Mind; and the majority of people, oblivious of the need for such inner ability, focus only outwardly on the result. "Pure" here equates to the verb form, meaning to "purify" the Mind of its attachments and vexations, its disputes and its perception of "me" versus others. This function of purifying the Mind is simultaneously Nirvana, enlightenment and Pure Land.

A Zen master once said, "I sought spring the entire day, but spring is nowhere to be found." Seeking enlightenment or the Pure Land is like seeking spring, which is unattainable outside your own mind. Once Master Mi Yun was presented with a portrait of himself as a gift. He wrote on the portrait the following commentary: "Neither traceable, nor paintable, to draw [my image] is like blind people touching the elephant; it would be better to burn the drawing and feel my true face with my own hands." Zen masters always try to illuminate the Mind by contemplating appearances, seeing the essence through the phenomena. To know your look, you only need to touch your face. Always look inward, not outward.

Liberty comes not from the pursuit or practice of gaining something but instead from letting go. A mind filled with disturbances cannot be free. The Sutra of Perfect Enlightenment states, "Moving eyes can shake peaceful water," meaning the view is clouded when the mind is not calm. "I sought spring the entire day, but spring is nowhere to be found; my straw sandals traced all over the cloud-covered hills. Upon returning home, I gave a plum flower a light-hearted sniff; only then I realized that spring has been in full blossom." Seeking enlightenment outside yourself will never bring success. Instead, simply let go of attachment; the Pure Land is already within you. Look within, cast the light inward and you will discover what you seek, for the Mind is already there.

Cultivation leads to freedom, enlightenment and eventually to becoming Buddha. However, we cannot become the Sakyamuni Buddha. We can instead become our own Buddha. Pure thought resonates with Pure Land. The transformation of attachments into pure thoughts and future karma into pure karma is the way to usher in the Pure Land. According to Zen Buddhism, the Mind is Buddha and a pure mind is the Pure Land, so all cultivations start from the Mind.

Master Wu Ye, of Fenzhou, spared no effort in his teaching of the Nirvana Sutra. Having heard of Master Ma Zu's outstanding Zen practice, he decided to pay a visit. Seemingly impressed by Wu Ye's robust physique and sonorous voice, Master Ma Zu said, "What a magnificent prayer hall, but why is there no Buddha inside?" No sooner had Ma Zu finished than Wu Ye was on his knees, saying, "I studied all the scriptures of the Triyana [the three vehicles], but the Zen idea of 'the Mind is Buddha' is beyond my grasp."

Ma Zu replied, "This mind of not-knowing is itself the Buddha, nothing else." Still confused, Wu Ye asked, "Then, what is the secret Mind seal the patriarch brought from the West?" Ma Zu simply said, "You are rather disturbed at this moment. Leave now, and come back another time." The moment Wu Ye turned to leave, Master Ma Zu called out, "Venerable…" Wu Ye stopped and turned back to face Ma Zu, who then continued, "…is what?" And that moment Wu Ye became enlightened.

Later Master Wu Ye became the abbot of a monastery where he taught his disciples nothing but this: "Do not have erroneous thinking." Without erroneous thinking, peace, truth and enlightenment will come. Distinctions between Zen and Pure Land are erroneous thinking; to distinguish among Theravada, Mahayana and the Esoteric teaching is no different than distinguishing between a thought to laugh and a thought to cry: Both are of little significance. They are simply functions of the Mind; the Mind itself is what is important.

Every cultivation must be rooted in the Mind. Erroneous discriminations obstruct the path to the Mind and the Truth. The Mind, illuminating inwardly, is there all along, clear and bright. Take one step at a time to meditate, chant and practice Zen, and bear in mind that these steps are for the purpose of eradicating false thinking. When attachments are shattered, the inner light will shine forth. There is no need to spin around within these false discriminations of the mind. Simply cultivate the fundamentals, in which one measure of effort begets a measure of harvest. This principle is simple but true.

> Crops are not aware of working the field;
> Carpenter builds a bed for himself to sleep in;
> Raindrops fall upward to the blue sky;
> I live on the south bank of the Yellow River.

3 EXPERIENCING THE NATURE OF LIFE: SUDDEN ENLIGHTENMENT VERSUS GRADUAL CULTIVATION

Master Xiang Lin had his name called for eighteen years;

Scholar Zhang Zhuo originally had no name;

Layman Pang Yun humbly walked the lake and river;

Master Long Tan glimpsed the spirit in the dragon.

Sudden Enlightenment Is the Recognition of the Original Mind

Life, in the purview of Buddhism, is by nature eternal. Other religions assert that human beings, not being the creators of their own lives, can only restore eternity through the return to God's domain. In Zen Buddhism, the Mind has always been. There is no reason or cause for it. The Mind simply exists, much like the essence of existence in philosophies or God, which exist without explanation.

Although the Mind has always been, erroneous beliefs keep it from manifesting its own eternal nature. To be free of birth and death, we must realize the Mind. But if, out of ignorance, we mistake our thoughts and body as "I," we then base our understanding on the false perception that existence is divided between mind and matter. Thus we obscure the true nature of life. The Hua-tou practice of Zen focuses on eliminating ego attachment and dispelling ignorance in order to reveal the source of life and its pure, selfless nature. The

Mind essence has no form and therefore can only be known through silent impression, but the Mind is alive in its awakening nature. It is able to give rise to functions and manifest all appearances so we can hear, see, feel and know. Everything one hears, sees, feels and knows is but the result of the functions of the Mind.

Attachment clings to the Mind the way dust clings to a mirror, obscuring and distorting the image. A common person's mind is by nature as clean and pure as a saint's mind. The two differ only in the extent of their erroneous attachments, much as the amount of dust on the mirror may vary. However, a mirror covered with dust can still reflect: "The saints are enlightened and function with clarity of mind; the mundane are perplexed and function with a tarnished mind." A saint's mind is clear due to its lack of erroneous beliefs; a mundane person's mind is full of heavy, complicated opinions, distorting the truth. Such heavy habitual tendencies are the manifestation of attachment, which tarnishes the mind.

Each of the world's seven billion people has a mind. In other words, your way of creating thoughts through your attachment is only one out of seven billion ways. Consequently, everyone's appearance, habits and ways of thinking vary, reflecting how each mind works in a unique, confined way. The Mind essence is free of ego and appearances, like the void with limitless capacity. Appearances created by the Mind can fill the void, while in a mundane mind the limitless capacity of the void is obstructed by insignificant, erroneous beliefs.

The function of the Mind not only determines the direction that your life and its various appearances will take, but the environment thus manifested also shows the inevitable consequence of the Mind's function. For instance, you may be reading my words in the initial moment your eyes pass over them, but then you understand me according to your habitual ways. You mold my words into your habitual pattern of thinking. People's various prejudices give them different emotions and understandings by subconsciously placing the facts into pre-existent molds created by their own attachments.

People see the world through the lenses of their habits. When confronted with challenges, they hope the world will change to suit their habits. They miss the point that it is they themselves who must change. If you remain the same, how could the world change? If your comprehension and interpretation of people, events and things are so tainted with habitual thinking that you simply cannot think outside the box, you will remain in the familiar prison of your own ideas. Even now, you are interpreting and discriminating my teaching through habitual thoughts. You are taking these thoughts as "I," as is your habit. But it is by doing so that people become confused and lose touch with the source of life.

Be it attained by sudden enlightenment or through gradual cultivation, the destination is enlightenment; the state in which one dispels ego and sees the Mind. Because this experience seems to occur through an instantaneous shift, it is called sudden enlightenment. Zen Master Dong Shan came to study with Master Yun Men. Yun Men asked him, "Where do you come from?" He replied, "Cha Du, west of the river." Yun Men then asked, "Where did you spend summer?" He said, "In Baoci, Hunan, south of the lake." Yun Men further asked, "When did you depart from there?" He said, "August twenty-fifth."

Yun Men said, "I'll give you three rounds of blows." The day after, Dong Shan went to Yun Men and asked, "Yesterday I was given three rounds of blows. May I ask what my fault was?" Yun Men said, "You good-for-nothing rice bag! So, this is how you wander about, west of the river and south of the lake!?" Upon hearing this, Dong Shan came to a powerful enlightenment experience, so he said, "From now on I'll live in remote places, store not a single kernel of rice, plant not a single patch of vegetables, receive people from all around, pull out the nails and remove the wedges, shedding the hat of fatty grease and clothes of foul ignorance, and get to the core of this nakedly exposed, carefree monk. Would not that be fantastic?" Yun Men simply said, "Your body is but the size of a coconut, but your mouth surely opened up magnificently."

Upon hearing the words, "You good-for-nothing rice bag! So, this is how you wander about west of the river and south of the lake!?" Master Dong Shan instantly let go of his ego and opened up the capacity of his mind. Therefore, his mouth opened up very wide. As shown in this story, the purpose of sudden enlightenment is to recognize the illusory nature of "I" and recover the Buddha nature of the Mind. In that moment of sudden enlightenment, it is possible to recognize the primordial Mind and its formless, selfless nature. The Mind is formless, but it possesses the innate capacity to function.

A factory produces many products; a mind creates many thoughts and manifestations. Because each person's mind creates thoughts, those thoughts and appearances are part of that person. Most people, however, only identify a small fraction of the Mind's function as self. A happy thought may be followed by a troublesome thought, which may be followed by a sad thought. The thinker subconsciously identifies himself with these thoughts, unable to recognize that the Mind is the true self of eternal life. This subconscious state is called ignorance.

When a person who has not cultivated his thoughts becomes attached to an angry thought, he believes he is angry. The habitual labeling of thoughts as self keeps one stuck in the erroneous notion of "I," which lives a life of turbulence as it rises and falls with external circumstances. It is said that the attachment to "I" is the root of birth and death. The continuous process of grasping thought and identifying the thought as self is the mark of a deluded mind. Because this "I" is always fluctuating and changing, it is not unlike a restless monkey that spends its rootless life swaying from one tree to another, spending all its time drifting from tree to tree without ever living on solid ground.

This "swaying"—the belief that we are our thoughts, whereby we grasp one thought after another—is called *samsara,* or transmigration. It is an ever-changing circulation between one appearance and another, and between life and death. Such a life is full of upheaval, confusion and aimless bustling. It moves the person who lives this way further and further away from the Mind of emptiness, peace, purity and freedom from ego. According to the Contemplation of Mind Ground Sutra, "Sentient beings transmigrate here and there among the six realms of existence, like an endlessly turning wheel." This describes the process, with neither a beginning nor an end, in which the mind grasps appearances and thoughts while the thoughts and appearances continue to change.

Your reality is the result of ever-changing conditions and karma: The moment an appearance or manifestation is created, it disappears. This is the nature of existence. If attachment to the self is not destroyed, a person cannot recognize his true nature and the emptiness of the innate Mind. People who seek truth outside the Mind only find the appearances of the Mind. This is much like a worker who goes to a factory each day to pick up goods without ever setting foot inside the workshop. One day he enters the workshop and discovers the vast capacity of the factory to produce. Only if life is able to produce the desired results will it be lively, colorful and free.

The continual mistaking of thoughts as oneself can self-perpetuate to the point that it becomes an ego-expanding habit. Human beings can control some thoughts but not others. Whether or not a person is able to control his or her thoughts, he or she basically believes that thoughts are the inner self, and he or she has separated other manifestations of the whole as the outer self. Karmic conditioning brings forth the habit of searching for truth outside the Mind. It hinders the fulfillment of life's potential, which is far greater than most people realize.

Sudden enlightenment means clearing the mind of ego attachment to recover the true Mind. Without a clear Mind, the issue of life and death cannot be settled. It is an issue that causes confusion and obstacles for the Mind. Because thoughts and phenomena change constantly, a life that is dependent on thoughts and phenomena will suffer. The chief purpose of Buddhist cultivation is to be free of life and death, at which one can help others do the same. To be free of life and death is to realize the true Mind and find the source of life. Being dependent on phenomena is like being permanently dependent on welfare: All a person can do is to take what she is given. Such a life is utterly passive. An enlightened mind leaves passivity behind, goes back to the source, and lives a life that is creative and proactive.

The Mind itself is not limited to specific perceptions; it is our attachment that restricts the perceptions of the Mind. It reduces the inherently free, flexible Mind into a fixed, egocentric mind that is unable to recognize its essential nature. Cultivation depends on enlightenment, which is the recognition of the Tao. This, in turn, is the Mind's unlimited essential nature and capacity; its ability to manifest anything you want to manifest. Thus you become increasingly habituated to whatever you habitually manifest. Once you recognize the Tao, you can cultivate according to the Tao and then manifest the Tao in your life.

The nature of the Mind is free of "I," but to be free of "I" does not mean nothingness. Instead, it is real freedom with neither artificiality nor dependence on external conditions. Master Wu Ye of Fenzhou, prior to his passing, gave the following instruction to his disciples: "Your Buddha nature of seeing, hearing and knowing is as everlasting as the great void, beyond arising and dissolution. The essence of any state is emptiness whereby not a single appearance can be grasped. Not knowing this, the ignorant one ends up in a state of illusion, trapped in transmigration. Each of you should understand that the Mind has always been and is not created. Like a diamond, it cannot be destroyed. All appearances, like shadows and sounds, are not concrete, for as the scriptures put it, 'Only this one essence is true; all dualities are unreal. Always know that all is void; not a single thing should be taken to heart.' This teaching embodies the function of Buddha's Mind, so you must all practice diligently."

The nature of the Mind is not anger, frustration, erroneous thoughts or suffering, even though it has the ability to create them. Instead, it transcends all the relativistic concepts of the world; it is a wondrous emptiness that gives birth to everything, not a dead void of nothingness. It is not the appearances of men, women, adults or children, but it can manifest all of them. This ever-changing function of the Mind is impermanent, subject to arising and dissolution. It is not the source itself but is a result of conditioned karma. However, because the ability to rise above the material world relies on the true emptiness of the Mind, the material and the Mind cannot be separated.

Theravada Buddhism teaches the concepts of "suffering, emptiness, impermanence and non-self." Our world is full of suffering, such as in the cycle of birth, aging, disease and death; the suffering of parting from one's beloved; the suffering of meeting with those we resent; the suffering of the instability of the five aggregates; and the suffering of fruitless pursuit. Suffering is the result of attachment, which grasps the ups and downs of the fickle appearances within which there is no real self. Accordingly, Theravada Buddhism advocates cultivation practices whose aim is to eradicate attachment in order to end suffering. Mahayana Buddhism shares this idea in that Bodhisattvas use their own suffering and the sufferings of others to inspire and help all beings attain Nirvana.

Mahayana Buddhism has the concepts of "eternity, joy, self and purity." Why does it talk about eternity while the Theravada traditions emphasize impermanence? Impermanence applies only to the momentary change of appearances. However, your ability to hear sound does not disappear with the fading of the sound. The ability to hear is everlasting, while the sound heard is the result of the ever-changing function of the Mind. Here, eternity refers to the everlasting creativity of the Mind, which is constantly generating dependently arising impermanent functions. Thus the eternity of Mahayana and the impermanence of Theravada are not contradictory. One refers to the nature of appearances, and the other refers to the nature of the Mind.

Why does Mahayana acknowledge the self? It is because the self that Theravada works to eliminate is not the true self but a false one comprised of thoughts, habits and appearances, which are only temporary functions of the true self. The nature of the Mind is emptiness and lacks self: It has no existence in terms of form or appearance. The selfless Mind, contingent upon conditions, gives rise to selfless functions. The Mind and the phenomenon are both selfless. This selfless collective of the formless Mind, its functions and appearances is what the Diamond Sutra refers to as the "One Composite." The One Composite is the true emptiness and the transcendental existing self as opposed to a false egoistic self, which is merely part of the "I versus others" duality. This selfless Mind embodies not only the appearances of all shapes and forms but also the formless essence. The non-self in Theravada Buddhism refers to the dependently arising appearances that cannot be substantiated, while the self of Mahayana Buddhism is the Collective, which encompasses the formless essence and all appearances. Thus the Mahayana concept of self is not in conflict with Theravada's concept of non-self.

Some people believe that because sudden enlightenment is a Zen concept, a person who is not a Zen disciple does not need to pursue it. You may choose not to use the term "sudden enlightenment," but to attain enlightenment one must break through this conditioned attachment because it is an indispensable condition of freedom from the circle of life and death. For instance, imagine that you are studying in the best preparatory school, but what matters in the end is not how excellent the school is but whether or not you can gain admission to a prestigious college. Similarly, it is meaningless to claim that your method and practice are direct, effective, most precious and unique, or to label them as being derived from a particular sect or an inheritance. If you do not let go of attachment and see the Tao, all your claims will be irrelevant.

Tao is *Bodhi*, the perfect wisdom; it is the functioning principle of the Mind. In the true void, different functions of the mind lead to different directions and paths. While the paths differ, they all arise from the same essential nature of the Mind. A calm, selfless mind works along a clean, clear path, or Bodhi. The Tao developed from a polluted ego and mind is a human path, not a Buddha path, and the Tao developed through greed is the path of the hungry ghost realm.

Bodhi Tao results from the function of a pure mind. Under such a function, the true emptiness and appearances arising from it are not one or two separate appearances but a whole. Neither do they constitute mind within and appearances without. This all-encompassing state of the non-duality of functions and essence is called the *Prajna* (wisdom) function. Zen Master Yang Shan paid a visit to Master Gui Shan. He asked, "Where does Buddha reside?" Gui Shan replied, "Use the transcendental thoughtless-thought; illuminate the eternal essence of the Mind. Where thoughts end, return to the great source and reside with the Buddha nature. Essence and functions are not-two, and that is where the true Buddha resides." Upon hearing this, Yang Shan attained sudden enlightenment.

The appearance of Prajna—or the highest wisdom—is no less than the appearance of "the other shore," or Nirvana. The Platform Sutra of the Sixth Patriarch states, "Prajna takes no shape and form other than the Wisdom Mind itself." Prajna comes from a pure, ego-free mind, where there is no distinction of "me versus others," inside versus outside, active versus passive, the void versus existence or life versus death. This state is clearly illustrated in the Avatamsaka Sutra: "A thousand-year span of time is inseparable from the thought of this present moment; limitless realms are not separated from the self by even a hair-width gap." All functions operate within the Mind. When the attachments are removed to reveal the reality, this state is referred to as the emergence of wisdom. This state is the inseparable, mutually penetrating Hua-Yen dharma realms of the One Composite, from which vanish all distinctions of "me" and "others," inside and outside, and void and appearances.

Each of us has different karma. To live in different places is already a manifestation of karma. Different thoughts and appearances are also expressions of karma. Because karma is the only reflection and basis of your current life, you can only free yourself from the standpoint of your karma, because karma is the sole basis upon which your life can unfold. For example, if arrival at a lecture hall is called liberation, then the path each person takes to come to liberation will be different. There are different paths, methods, times and directions by which you travel to arrive at the hall, because each of you has a different karma. Each life is different.

You have your own body, thoughts and methods, and other people have theirs. Whatever method you employ, it must take you from your unique existence back to the Mind of emptiness and purity. It has been stated: "There are different methods for appropriate situations, but the only way is to return to Nirvana." Having returned to Nirvana, there are no two ways but only the way of the universal truth.

Zen Master Chang Qing studied Zen under the guidance of the masters Xue Feng and Xuan Sha. He had worn down seven meditation cushions. One day, as he rolled up the curtain, Chang Qing came to a sudden enlightenment and said, "All wrong, all wrong. I roll up the curtain and see the world. Someone asks me what I have seen, and I pick up the duster to hit him." Master Xue Feng overheard the verse and went to tell Master Xuan Sha, "He is enlightened." Still not convinced, Master Xuan Sha wanted to test Chang Qing again. Therefore, Master Xue Feng asked him to say again in front of everyone what he had understood. At this request, Chang Qing composed the following verse: "All appearances reveal this singular body; it only becomes real when oneself experiences it thus. In the past I searched up and down along the paths, but today I realize the search is like ice among fire."

The Mind gives rise to the functioning collective—the One

Composite of all functions—which is inseparable from the Mind, whose nature is emptiness. The Mind is inseparable from the myriad manifestations, and the myriad manifestations are revealed by the singular entity that is the Mind. There is nothing else but the myriad manifestation of appearances that form an inseparable whole. Thus we have the statement, "From all appearances comes One." The unity of a person's mind and its reality can only be experienced by that individual. One's efforts prior to the attainment of Nirvana are akin to "searching up and down the paths," as one wanders restlessly from one approach to the next. Up to enlightenment, the maze of erroneous thinking is merely the tip of the iceberg. However, once one is enlightened it becomes possible to fully realize the error of previous understanding, and all erroneous beliefs dissolve like "ice among fire."

Even After Sudden Enlightenment, Gradual Cultivation Is Still Necessary

One has no choice, prior to Nirvana, but to cultivate and develop methods of enlightenment based on the foundation of his karma. Every method is unique and has its own merit. Theravada, Mahayana and the Esoteric practice have their own karmas and particular teachings. Only you can create your path to freedom based on your own karma; no one can attain freedom for you, nor can one person attain freedom based on another's karma.

It is appropriate to follow a particular sect whose methods and theories have been developed based on the practitioner's karma, but this does not reveal the ultimate truth. The truth is not a shortcut method, nor can it be measured as slow or fast. Neither does it contain any sentimentality. The truth is universal and without exception. Contrary to the nature of truth, a common understanding formed out of different karmas, eras and beliefs is nothing more than a regionally specific education. It is not the truth. Therefore, be it Zen, Mahayana, Theravada or the Esoteric teaching, it is but a means of education arising from the different karmas of its followers and the shared, or group, karma. People may be taught to believe that what they learn is the only truth, but that is not necessarily so. Instead, it is just a common karma shared by a group of people.

The issue of life and death can never be resolved unless one eradicates attachment and returns to the purity of the Mind. Therefore, it matters little which spiritual tradition a person follows. The truth, without exception, is that different spiritual teachings and methods are simply manifestations of different kinds of karma and attachments in the minds of people. No matter which school you attend, what education you receive or what shortcut you take, all are in vain if you do not complete your curriculum in the cyclical school of birth and death. The purpose of your effort, no matter what means you use, is to return to the source of life.

Master Xiang Yan was originally Master Bai Zhang's disciple. Although he was very intelligent, he had not attained enlightenment. After the passing of Master Bai Zhang, he went to follow Master Gui Shan. Gui Shan said to him, "I heard that when you were a disciple of Bai Zhang you could give ten answers when asked for one and give one hundred when asked for ten. It shows that you are very smart and witty with your discriminating mind, which is actually the root of birth and death. Now, tell me in one sentence what it was like before you were born to your parents." Xiang Yan was very perplexed by the request. He went back to his room and re-read all the scriptures, but still he failed to find anything in relevance to Gui Shan's question. He sighed and said, "A painted pancake is not going to fill my stomach." Therefore, he pleaded with Gui Shan for the answer, but Gui Shan said, "If I told you, later you would resent me. After all, my answer is mine and could have nothing to do with you."

Xiang Yan then set fire to all his scriptures, saying, "I will learn no more dharma. I might as well spare my mind and spirit the trouble and become a simple monk." He tearfully bid Gui Shan farewell and later settled down at a farm that had once belonged to the Imperial Preceptor Hui Zhong. One day he was weeding and tossed aside a pebble that ended up hitting a piece of bamboo; at the sound of the pebble hitting the bamboo he was enlightened. He went home, bathed, lit incense and kowtowed toward the direction of Master Gui Shan, saying, "Master's mercy and grace to me are greater than that of my parents. Had you told me the answer, how would it have been possible for me to obtain this experience today?" He then composed the following verse:

> One strike, all knowledge is forgotten;
> No artifijicial cultivation is necessary after all.
> Every moment I uphold the ancient Way,
> Never retreating into silent stagnation.
> Nowhere shall I leave any trace;
> Virtue is beyond sound and form.

Everywhere those who have attained the Way,
All declare this to be the Ultimate Truth.
Intellectual understandings are all means—
Why bother carrying it with you all the time?

Enlightenment is returning to the source. So, why then is further cultivation necessary? Enlightenment is only a realization of the nature of the Mind. All beings have many habitual tendencies and attachments, so the elimination of ego attachment does not guarantee an automatic elimination of all habits. "Although sudden enlightenment ushers in the Buddha, habitual tendencies are deeply rooted; the wind has ceased, but there are still waves; the Essence has been revealed, but thoughts still intrude." Therefore, cultivation should continue well after enlightenment. The elder Zhaozhou achieved enlightenment as early as eighteen but continued his travel study into his eighties. Gradual cultivation after enlightenment involves efforts to retain the state of true emptiness and freedom from the ego in order to gradually dissolve all erroneous thinking and outward-seeking habits.

A person, prior to enlightenment, is like a homeless man wandering from one place to another and clinging to one thought after another. After enlightenment, the homeless man finds and returns home, but it takes some tidying up before it feels like a perfect place. How could anyone live in a place that is still dusty and dirty? Even after the elimination of ego attachment, its shadow will continue to act up where the attachment had once been most prominent. Therefore, we need to cultivate ceaselessly before and after enlightenment, passing what Zen Buddhism calls the initial barrier, the double barrier and the stubborn barrier. The last of these is the final stage, where ego attachments are completely eradicated and will never again manifest themselves.

The story of the Sixth Patriarch Master Hui Neng, of the Tang Dynasty, is familiar to many. Due to his accumulated wisdom from previous incarnations, Hui Neng was able to achieve enlightenment when he, a mere firewood logger, heard the Diamond Sutra for the very first time. However, because he had passed only the initial barrier, his realization was not yet complete. Upon the recommendation of the Diamond Sutra chanter, Hui Neng traveled all the way from Guangzhou to Huangmei County, Hubei, in order to visit the Fifth Patriarch Hong Ren. Along the way, he endured all kinds of hardships. At that time, Master Hong Ren had a disciple called Shen Xiu, who was admired by many for his diligence. Despite that diligence, Shen Xiu had not obtained enlightenment. One day, Master Hong Ren asked his disciples to compose verses, hoping they would shed light on which one of his disciples had realized the wisdom essence and was worthy of his mantle and alms bowl or, in other words, his legacy. Shen Xiu immediately wrote this verse on the wall: "My body is the Bodhi tree and my mind the bright-mirror terrace; I dust them day and night, making sure that no dust remains."

It became obvious to Hui Neng, once he heard the verse, that the writer was not enlightened. He then wrote his own verse, which read, "Bodhi is no tree, and the bright mirror has no terrace; originally there was not a single object, so where would the dust cling?" Afterwards,

Hui Neng was summoned to Master Hong Ren's room. Then and there, the Fifth Patriarch started teaching him the Diamond Sutra. When it came to the sentence, "One's mind should function without abiding," Hui Neng became enlightened and said to the Master, "How could I have imagined that the Mind is by nature pure, beyond arising and dissolving, complete, immutable and omnipotent?" Hearing this, the Fifth Patriarch knew that Hui Neng had truly become enlightened to the primordial nature, so to him the patriarch passed his mantle and alms bowl.

Cultivation is a long process. It begins with the stage of developing the right understanding of the Tao, and it moves through the stage of identifying the method by which to practice the Tao; the stage of breaking attachment through the practice of the method and the attainment of enlightenment; the stage of post-enlightenment gradual cultivation; and the final stage, in which other beings are liberated. Every stage has its own unique distractions, landscape and view.

The great matter of life and death is considered resolved only when ego attachment no longer re-emerges, the habit of seeking truth outside the Mind vanishes and the Mind is in full harmony with its own nature, which is emptiness, Bodhi and Nirvana simultaneously. Zen Buddhism describes the Mind as a bull and the process of pursuing enlightenment as the search for the bull. Even if you catch the bull, it may still be wild and hard to control. The wild bull needs taming, but once tamed it will follow you wherever you go. Zen Buddhism calls a tamed mind "the white bull in the open space."

A person, once he has attained enlightenment, needs to spend time and effort to cultivate it as if it were a newborn that would perish without proper care and nourishment. This process is called *bao-ren*, or abiding, which means to maintain oneself firmly and permanently in the emptiness, wisdom and purity of the Mind. After Master Rui Yan attained enlightenment, each day he would ask himself, "How is the Master doing?" Then he would answer himself, "Stay alert and do not be deceived." This process is also called *guan-dai*, as if you are taking a child to the market and would therefore need to hold his hand *(dai)* and make sure he does not wander about *(guan)*. We need to do the same with the emptiness, the wisdom and the purity of the Mind, which are manifested through enlightenment while habitual tendencies and deluded thinking gradually dissolve.

Deluded thoughts may, however, emerge even after enlightenment. When that occurs, you must turn the light inward on yourself so that your mind is returned to the emptiness, awareness and clarity of the primordial Mind. The perpetuation of deluded thought is called *shi*, or consciousness; and the emptiness, awareness and clarity of the primordial Mind are collectively called *zhi*, or wisdom. Without enlightenment, one can only transform one type of consciousness into another but can never transform it into wisdom. The process of turning *shi* into *zhi*—transforming consciousness into wisdom—is called *bao-ren* in Zen Buddhism, and enlightenment is its prerequisite.

Bao-ren is an indispensable process, so it takes time. Moreover, the time that will be needed is dependent on the individual's karma, cultivation and amount of effort. Some enlightenment is able to eradicate somewhat deep attachments and false beliefs, because the person has the deep meditative power needed to gradually remove old habits from early on. Other enlightenment, however, simply manages to eradicate superficial, deluded beliefs. In that case, the person may have achieved a shallow enlightenment, largely due to wisdom and virtue gained from the past. Another may still have deep-rooted habits but lack meditative power and/or strong discipline. Under such circumstances, the process of *bao-ren* will be more arduous.

Eliminating Ego Attachment Through Sudden Enlightenment and Gradual Cultivation

Whether through sudden enlightenment or gradual cultivation, it is imperative to focus yourself in order to get rid of mundane habits and temperament and thereby open your heart as much as possible. Gradual cultivation means making step-by-step progress toward a lucid understanding of your true situation. This practice is necessary in order to put aside your myriad troubles; only through this approach can you become truly immune to negative influences. Why do we need gradual cultivation? It is because Rome was not built in a day and bad habits, which have been piled up layer after layer throughout a person's previous lives, cannot be easily cast away. The true nature of the Way may be understood instantly, but bad habits cannot be eliminated so quickly. Gradual cultivation is like filing away the rust to show the true light of the soul. Even if a person has attained enlightenment, gradual cultivation remains essential.

The great Master Zi-bo Zhen-ke, of the late Ming Dynasty, traveled the world with his sword when he was only seventeen years old. One night, it was raining very hard so he stayed in a temple. Then and there he heard the monks chanting the *Eighty-Eight Buddhas'*

Repentance. The very next day, he decided to become a monk. He had worked very hard after entering into monastic life. At one time he did not leave his room for half a year, and he lived in seclusion for three years. He then decided to travel the world in order to acquire knowledge and understand the great matter of life and death. At one point in his travels, he heard a monk reading the scholar Zhang Zhuo's poem. When the monk reached the phrase "to remove delusions but only gain illness, to strive for truth but only achieve deviance," Zi-bo Zhen-ke became confused. He said, "That is wrong. It should be no illness, no deviance." However, the monk replied, "You are wrong. He is right." Zi-bo Zhen-ke became even more confused. He then copied these two lines from the poem on the wall and meditated on them until his head and face were swollen. One day, as he ate, he was suddenly enlightened, and immediately the swelling disappeared from his face and head. This is a well-known case of gradual cultivation that resulted in sudden enlightenment.

It is of course necessary, before one attains sudden enlightenment, to have a method and guidance to follow for meditation and study. The purpose of Zen is, first of all, to realize the truth before everything else. It will not be possible to implement practice according to the Tao unless one understands the truth. Instead, any practice will be based merely on convenient means but not on the ultimate truth. Thus the right way of Zen practice is to first strive for enlightenment in order to practice the Tao. Before enlightenment, the goal of gradual cultivation is to attain enlightenment. The purpose of gradual cultivation after enlightenment is the maintenance and deepening of the realization of enlightenment. Practice is continued in order to eliminate all traces of ego attachment in the real nature of emptiness, awareness and clarity, and to let the real nature of emptiness, awareness and clarity persist moment by moment.

A person may, after enlightenment, continue to eliminate ego attachment using a convenient method based on subject/object duality. Because the nature of attachment, like the nature of dualistic practice, is illusory, using one illusion to dispel another illusion will return one to the ultimate. Therefore, after enlightenment you can continue the practice of *hua-tou*, the contemplation of the impurity of the body, visualization or the recitation of a mantra. These dualistic methods can still serve as antidotes to deeply rooted habits and attachments. Eventually, one can set aside such methods. As you withdraw from the use of these dualistic methods, you will return and abide in the self-nature, the emptiness, awareness and clarity that manifested during your enlightenment experience. In other words, you can simply abide in the self-nature and practice without separating from the emptiness, awareness and clarity. This type of practice is gradual, but nevertheless it is used only after one attains enlightenment.

The delusion of discrimination—which is also called attachment to phenomena—can sometimes occur after enlightenment. Additionally, there is the delusion of view, which is also called the attachment to ego. Whether the attachments are to phenomena or ego, they are dependent on the notion of "I" and differ only in terms of degree. They are conveniently categorized as the delusion of view, delusion of discrimination and delusion of fundamental ignorance. Ultimately, the issue of life and death cannot be resolved until every trace of "I"—or ego attachment—is eradicated. According to the Diamond Sutra, "If a Bodhisattva is thoroughly established in the state of selflessness: no self, no you, no beings and no time." This refers to the complete elimination of ego or self-attachment, which is the end of life and death. From this state of absolute selfless purity, practice the path of Bodhisattva and "cultivate all virtues without attachment." Because pure function begets a pure result, when the results are complete and perfected the practitioner manifests ultimate, unsurpassed equanimity and perfected awakening.

First, try to achieve the state of selflessness. If the function of your mind is not yet satisfactory, make the necessary correction to perfect every aspect until Buddhahood is ultimately achieved. This is a clear path of cultivation. Sudden enlightenment is the elimination of ego attachment. When your ego attachment is eliminated, you see the Tao. When you see the Tao, it is possible to cultivate it. When you cultivate the Tao to the point of complete selflessness— the eradication of every ego attachment and habitual tendency— you then attain the Tao. This is the order of cultivation. Prior to enlightenment, practice should be carried out in order to eliminate ego attachment. After enlightenment, gradual practice is for the purpose of abiding in the Tao. Gradual practice is still required after sudden enlightenment.

Theravada, Mahayana, Esoteric teachings and the various schools of Buddhism are merely convenient means because they are unique to each particular tradition. Each school and variation of Buddhism is a result that corresponds to the karmas of sentient beings. Because the karmic results of beings are all different from one another, there is nothing to compare. Inciting conflict among different schools of Buddhism is the same as stating that apples are not as sour as oranges and that oranges do not have the color of apples. Because different beings have different karmas, their results are different, and therefore the teachings that manifest them are also different. When your karma is as such, you have no choice but to encounter such method, ritual and teaching. It is essential that you eliminate your ego attachment from your existing karma in order to return to the self-nature. This is the purpose of the various spiritual teachings and traditions.

Any school of Buddhism you might practice is just a matter of convenience without the elimination of ego attachment and the enlightenment of the self-nature. Without returning to the origin, all your efforts will be in vain. As it is said, "Practice without the arising of Bodhicitta—Awakening Mind—is like farming without seeds." The Bodhicitta refers to the Mind of emptiness, awareness and clarity. The Bodhicitta is the primordial Mind: our primordial nature. Practice that is not based on the cause or the source is simply a fleeting phenomenon. Without removing the delusions of the external seeking mind, all existence is fleeting, impermanent and cyclical. Zen uses sudden enlightenment as a metaphor for the elimination of ego attachment. Enlightenment is a must because, without it, everything is delusory. Sudden enlightenment does not belong only to Zen. No one can do without it. It is the gate that stands between existing in life and death and moving beyond the cycle of life and death.

Sudden enlightenment is the realization of self-nature. Gradual cultivation serves to eliminate all ego attachments and habitual tendencies. No practice of any school of Buddhism can deviate from this principle. Without the elimination of ego attachment, the cycle of life and death will continue as another round of incarnation, in which the state of homeless wandering persists. Everyone should find a suitable method of practice and work on it continuously. Your practice is your own business, and accordingly your thoughts and karma are your own responsibility. It is not a problem that you might belong to one school of Buddhism or another. The mind of right-and-wrong making is the problem. Through your own karma, eradicate your attachment and then achieve freedom. Clearly, that is the way to proceed.

> The nature of the Mind is the point of enlightenment,
> The point of enlightenment is the root of the Mind.
> The source of the mind is the enlightenment of essence,
> An enlightened mind is clear and bright.
> With the most supreme stroke of luck of all times,
> Therefore we encounter today;
> Ba-ba wa-wa,
> In seamless harmony.

4 MIND IS BUDDHA

Long reed hidden in water to cover the trace
Heron fleeing, suspecting the hood of the reed boat.
Bright moon shining on the hidden herons ever bright
No need to borrow lanterns from the fisherman

Take Responsibility for the Life You Create

Each culture has its core philosophy, and the Zen philosophy of "Mind is Buddha" is the essential core value of Mahayana Buddhism. No matter the culture and ideology, it changes with the passing of time. The existence of history proves that everything is going through change every second. People grow. The relationships between people and everything else change as well. The environment is different now than it was in ancient times. Society undergoes the cycle of stability and turbulence. Countries and nations go through cycles of prosperity and decline. The earth and the universe are ever-changing.

Greed, hatred, ignorance, arrogance, doubts and misunderstanding in people's minds have resulted in stubborn predicaments and cyclic reincarnation in this ever-changing world. However, the Mind of all living creatures has the ability to create ever-changing phenomena. This ability is the source of life, and therefore it is constant. The myriad species and life forms are the results of karma arising from the Mind and its power to create. While we call the record of phenomenal transformation history, every form of life is created by the Mind.

Each of us thinks differently, and consequently the path of each life is bound to be different. Generally, a person's life path is guided by her unconscious pattern of thought. The Mind continuously and unconsciously creates an endless series of ever-changing phenomena. But when you come to the understanding of the Mind's essential nature, the unfolding of life is now initiated from the purity of the Mind. Thus you consciously create your reality. At this point in the state of your life, it can be said, "The Mind is the Buddha, and the moment of creation is the moment of dissolution."

Pure Mind begets Pure Land, but a defiled mind begets a defiled reality. This notion is not just a slogan. It is the principle of each individual taking responsibility for the life he has created, whether good or bad. Moreover, it is the everlasting universal truth. When the mind creates a thought of laughter, the corresponding facial expression and changes in the environment arise simultaneously, not as a sequence. Thought and the presentation of life are born together, being created and presented by the Mind.

Every second brings change to your thoughts and environment. Your mind—like everyone's—is filled with the thoughts and habits that you have created, and they are connected through attachment and taken to be "I." In reality, thoughts result from the habitual tendencies of the mind. Thoughts lead to actions, and actions have effects. The mind encompasses these effects, which then constitute a reality and influence their future development.

The nature of the Mind refers to the essence of the Mind. Therefore, the principle of cause and effect describes the form and function of the Mind. Essence, form and function are distinctions we use, for the sake of convenience, to describe various aspects of the wholeness of Mind. Essence means that the Mind is, by nature, pure. The ability to hear is always pure, and this pure source has the capacity to create everything in life. The clarity and distinctiveness of each sound you hear in fact comprise the manifestation, or the "form," created by the Mind. The functioning of the Mind is exemplified by its ability to hear various sounds and further create different phenomena.

Function must arise from the Mind, but form also emerges from the Mind. Essence is simply the original purity of the Mind. From the Mind arise functions such as thoughts, each of which assumes a form. Therefore, essence, form and function are simply three aspects of the Mind's functional presentation. They are not three disjointed entities. However, we cannot even say that form and function return to the essence. The truth is that form and function are already changes that occur within the essence: One is three, and three is one. All forms unfold in the void. Therefore, if the void is considered to be the essence, the phenomena in the void, such as houses, cars and environment, represent changes in the essence. When function changes, the essence and form change as well. The void and phenomena change together. There is no relationship of master to slave in terms of change and its initiation. The two are of a single origin.

True Emptiness and Existence Are One

The statement, "Mind and phenomenon are one," is another

way to describe the workings of the Mind. Consequently, Mind is the essence of the true Mind. Mind and phenomenon are simply two sides of the same coin, or life in its totality. The true Mind is "not-two." Not-two is neither one nor two. The nature of the true Mind can be understood as when one thing merges with another and becomes one. The true, unchanging essence of the Mind has the ability to simultaneously manifest phenomena. When this function of the Mind is at work, mind and phenomenon mutually penetrate and merge as "not-two," being neither one nor two.

Imagine that I clap my hands and you hear the sound. Do you hear it because your mind runs toward the sound or because the sound falls upon your ears? It is neither. The mind and phenomenon resonate with each other and arise simultaneously. The true Mind's ability to hear already exists. The moment the sound is heard is also the moment at which the true Mind's unchanging essence authentically presents the sound, simultaneously creating it in the moment. It is neither one nor two, nor is it before or after. The Mind intrinsically functions this way, presenting the results that correspond to its current functioning.

Dharma comes from the Mind. To practice Buddhism is to know how to benefit yourself and others without straying from the nature of the Mind. The nature of the Mind manifests equality, meaning that which we call the equality of emptiness, equality of enlightenment and equality of clarity. Equality means freedom from attachment, just as the Mind, whose nature is true emptiness, will not keep within it the sound of a single word once it is heard. The only things a deluded mind can keep are useless and superficial thoughts, not those spontaneously arising and dissolving, in essence as in function.

"Mind is Buddha" can also be understood as "true emptiness, transcendental existence." "True emptiness, transcendental existence" is the actual relationship between life's phenomena and their source. This is the understanding of the Mind from its two functional perspectives. Why can we hear different sounds at different times and in different places? It is because the nature of the Mind is pure, uncontaminated, true emptiness. That is why the Mind can dissolve as it functions and function as it dissolves. It is why the Mind can manifest transcendental existence in phenomena, doing so in response to various conditions of time and space while presenting reality as it is and being aware of reality as it is.

Emptiness and existence are non-dualistic; they are not separate. The Heart Sutra states, "form is emptiness, emptiness is form," and accordingly the phenomena of form occur because the Mind reveals them through its nature of true emptiness. However, the Mind's formlessness is revealed through the phenomena of form. Emptiness and form are not-two, so it is merely for the sake of convenience that we refer to them as being separate. The intrinsic nature of the Mind is emptiness, which is able to manifest all existence.

The Mind creates all dharma. The essence of the Mind is emptiness with neither attachment nor form. The essence of the Mind is broad and limitless, and everything is contained within it. The mind contains everything but is attached to nothing, and consequently every moment is both existence and emptiness. Each moment is creation and dissolution.

We can see mountains, oceans, the earth, cars coming and going, phenomena of all colors and forms, but all these phenomena can be gathered and traced to the nature of the form-seeing mind. From an existential perspective, vexations can never be Bodhi. To smile is not to cry, even though smiling and crying are functions of the Mind. Examining this concept more deeply, we can understand that even though we have attachment and fanciful thoughts, our mind neither increases nor decreases. Each human being has the ability to make his own karma. This ability will not diminish because an ordinary person has vexations, nor will it increase if he reaches enlightenment and becomes a saint. Ordinary people are spellbound but not lost. The spell is not real but is instead created through one's attachment.

Vexations and *Bodhi*, when viewed from the intrinsic nature of the mind, originate from a common source. The source that creates Bodhi is the same one that creates the vexations. When you see this, you will understand that merging, compatibility and unification abide within the Pure Mind. Furthermore, you will comprehend the essential non-duality of objects and beings. At this point, dilemmas in your life will be resolved. You will return to the source of life to create new phenomena, and you will put an end to the problems of duality.

If you can rid your mind of the habit of attachment, the corresponding karmic conditions will change the corresponding phenomena for the better because you will enhance the mind's ability to create. Such karma will always be better than that which is created by a mind filled with vexations. If you give rise to a thought of smiling while crying, are you not letting go of crying? As soon as a thought appears, the corresponding karma also appears. Thought is the focal point of the mind's functioning. It organizes the existential world, whereby cause and effect appear simultaneously. We simply assert that cause precedes effect for the sake of convenience. The "cause" in the so-called cause and effect can also be understood as "Buddha"—the essence of the mind in "Mind is Buddha"—while the "effect" is the form to which the mind gives rise, and it is "mind."

Mind is innate, whether it is deluded or enlightened. Every instant of life is a reflection of the principle that "Mind is Buddha." There is no Buddha that is not Mind, nor is there Mind that is not Buddha. Most people are deluded because they do not know the effect of the mind in the construct "Mind is Buddha." Saints are enlightened because they can return the effect of mind to the essence of Buddha at any instant, so they can perfectly practice "Mind is Buddha" and reveal the true substance of Mind. If practitioners understand the reason behind the statement, "Mind is Buddha," their efforts will not be in vain. If they can achieve a deep understanding of the statement, "Mind is Buddha," they will have wisdom and become free from the cycle of birth and death. The way of the Bodhisattva is to put "Mind is Buddha" into practice. To perfect "Mind is Buddha" is to become Buddha.

Winter plum, a little red dot in white snow
Sometimes there are flowers, sometimes not
Going home I look back and see all the leaves have fallen
Another blanket of snow descends and covers my track

5 TURN YOUR THOUGHTS AROUND AND CHANGE YOUR LIFE

Branches fall from iron tree and reveal the sky

Spoiled orange vainly occupies this year's spring

Carp fight to transform at the mouth of the dragon gate

Burn up its tail and leap, turning heaven and earth

The Purpose of Practice Is to Master Every Thought

Life is elevated and improved, and the mind is mastered, through practice. If the mind cannot be controlled, there will be problems and vexations. Thus the fundamental purpose of practice is to master the mind so you can take care of your thoughts in every moment. The Mind can, at every moment, manifest the phenomena of what you see and hear. If your mind is not in control, you will not be able to master your phenomena in life, nor will the mind's ability to know be mastered.

The phenomena of this instant include thought, body, environment, feeling and relationship. What exists at this instant is the karma created by your mind. However, your mind can only reveal your own karma. It cannot reveal someone else's. Your favorable state shows the responsibility you have over your karma, and that is why it is revealed as favorable. In the opposite case, when your mind creates unfavorable karma, the phenomena it reveals will also be unfavorable. If you do not want these phenomena, your mind must act to create a new one so that the karma and corresponding phenomena can change.

All phenomena change instantaneously, because the Mind creates different effects. At the moment the mind creates an effect, the effect changes and disappears. Moreover, the moment a phenomenon exists, it changes and disappears. This relationship indicates that life's source is pure and untainted. Its nature is empty, eternally free.

The Fourth Zen Patriarch Dao Xin went to visit the Third Patriarch Seng Can. The Fourth Patriarch said to the Third Patriarch, "Please be kind and merciful, and show me the way toward liberation." The Third Patriarch said, "Who tied you down?" In response, the Fourth Patriarch said, "Nobody tied me up." The Third Patriarch said, "If no one has tied you up, why are you looking for liberation?" You do not have to seek freedom, because you are already free. Try to think: Who tied you down? Was it your parents? Was it your children? If you put someone in your mind, that individual has effectively tied you down. The mind is like an empty basket. If you put a piece of clothing in the basket, there will be clothing in the basket, and if you put eggs in the basket there will be eggs in the basket.

The Confucian school also talked about the "made-mind" which, it explained, has a bias. The made-mind maintains a view of itself, from itself. The unenlightened person uses his or her made-mind to judge, thinking everything is just as what he sees, hears and knows. Unless you empty your mind and give up your made-mind, the phenomena that appear at every instant will not be real. The mind will retain no form, because it is always pure, empty and spotless.

Can you hang a nail in empty space? No, it is not possible. No matter what you do, no matter how you reveal mountains, seas and earth, you can only do so outside of emptiness. Emptiness represents intrinsic freedom, signifying that the real substance of the Mind is free of vexation and attachment. At the same time a sound exists, it changes and disappears, but the Mind's ability to hear with absolute clarity remains. This is what intrinsic freedom means.

If we can give up attachments, we will be free. Even if you cannot let go of vexations and attachments, your mind remains unconditionally free. Empty space will not become dirty if you place a bucket of dirt in it. Instead, it will remain empty. Empty space will not smell nice if you put a fragrant flower in it, because it has no smell in essence. You will not be able to pollute your mind's intrinsic freedom even if you try, because it is always free and pure. Give up your attachments, and your intrinsic freedom will appear.

If attachments exist, they will always have corresponding forms. People hold onto their point of view and think, "This has to be this, and that has to be that." However, while the true substance of the Mind is without form, it can reveal the form that the Mind has created. At any instant the Mind can reveal the form it creates, but the real substance of the Mind does not have this form. As the Third Patriarch Xun Can said, "Nobody tied you down." If you do not throw vexations into your mind, you will be free. The Mind, in and of itself, is clear and free.

Vexations, attachments and pain are self-inflicted, as are good karma and bad karma. Another person's karma will not affect you, nor can your karma become somebody else's. To practice means, first of all, to take responsibility for the burden of your karma. After all, you have no choice and there is no escape. The karma you create is the form revealed by your mind. The practitioner should not ask why things have happened this way or why disasters have befallen him, but instead he should ask why he has created this karma. The mind is the source of all problems, and all your problems are created by you. You are the one who thinks like this. You are the one who has a particular illness, a vexation or a problem with other people. Therefore, only you can resolve it.

The phenomena in each person's life are unique, because they are self-created. The way you look is created by your mind. If you have a kind, compassionate mind, you will naturally appear kind and compassionate. If you do not have a lot of wisdom, you will appear a bit daft. If you are irascible, you will appear angry. If you are stubborn and cannot easily turn your thoughts, this will be reflected in your appearance. That is why a fortune-teller can discern your personality based on your appearance. Your relationship with other people is your creation. You have ordered and organized a unique way of dealing with other people; you have chosen the people you would meet and where, and you have created the earth and the changes that will take place.

People find themselves in difficult circumstances of their own creation. They cannot move but only remain stationary, neither advancing nor retreating. Actually, the solution to the problem lies within their minds. What has not been created will not manifest. If the mind is not mastered, problems will occur in life. However, if you gain mastery of the mind, your life on earth will be happy and perfect, and consequently you can make efforts to attain enlightenment.

A lay practitioner wanted to buy a dharma instrument. He asked, "If I buy this instrument, do I have to hold it in my hand and visualize while I chant?" He was told, "My kind brother, when you visualize, just visualize. When you chant, there is no need to hold an instrument." Everything takes concentration and focus. If the teacher is talking and you are chanting, then where is your mind? If your mind is on chanting, it is not on listening; but if your mind is on listening, it is not on chanting. So, why chant? To chant for yourself is better than having someone chant for you, even ten thousand times. A thousand soldiers and ten thousand horses will not be able to turn a single thought for you. If you can give rise to a turning thought, then heaven and earth will open wide. If you cannot, they will be closed and you will perceive only darkness.

The important thing about practice is the mind. You must be the master of your own mind. If not, ten Buddha-chanting machines will not do you any good. It would be heresy to seek truth outside the Mind. Practice is "real guns and real bullets." It is not covering yourself with sutras or staying at home and chanting all day long. Practice means having mastery of the mind in every moment so as to clearly know each thought and rid yourself of vexations. To practice is to be the master of your own mind everywhere, in every thought and every moment. Otherwise, you will never be able to look at things clearly. Without practice, you will never be able to contemplate your problems and understand them. When you are having problems in life, do not look for answers outside yourself. Close your eyes and look at your thoughts. See how your mind works.

Someone once asked me, during a lecture, whether personal hobbies are considered attachment. I responded by saying he first needed to understand the Mind. Because it is the center and source of our lives, the Mind manifests itself in every aspect of our individual lives. If you are unaware of the nature and function of the Mind, you will create appearances in accordance with self-centered emotions and opinions. Therefore your appearance, relationships, and other aspects of your life and personality reveal where your attachment and biases lie.

A fearful mind can only create a fearful body and environment. It cannot manifest good health. A mind obsessed with the fear of losing a person or a prized possession cannot truly be with that person or that treasured possession, because the foundation is based on fear. Every positive relationship in life is intrinsically liberated, while only a mind that is free of negativity and in accordance with the nature of emptiness can create health, wealth and happiness. A mind that is not in accordance with emptiness can only create phenomena according to what it contains. A fearful mind creates more fear, a sorrowful mind creates more sorrow, and a dispute-filled mind creates more disputes.

One person cannot let go but desperately wants to do so. Another has a fearful mind but longs for fear-free relationships. Thus we have a paradox. However, if you can make yourself sick, you should be able to nurture yourself back to health. If you can create a poor relationship, you should be able turn the relationship around. The key is to know the root of the problem. Your mind is pivotal in this respect. The individual's mind is the source of illness and poor relationships. The failure to understand the Mind and how the desired reality is manifested—the condition of wanting but being unable to achieve—keeps most people trapped in their dilemmas.

Practitioners want spiritual realization and results, while non-practitioners want lives of health and happiness. Many people in the West believe the purpose of life is love. To those people, I ask the following question: How long can you love your parents, spouse or children? If this is your purpose, you cannot fulfill it. With all the erroneous beliefs, opinions and frustration in your mind, you are not the master of your own mind. Should not you have a smaller ego, less vexation and more wisdom in order to achieve your goal?

Many people believe that mind cultivation is a strictly religious matter of the monastics. Such people may assert that the purpose and significance of their life should be defined from the perspective of the mundane. If you say the purpose of life is love, then I encourage you to love yourself, your parents, your children and the people all around you. However, in order to do so your mind must also be flexible, healthy and kind. In that sense, the purpose of spiritual practice perfectly matches the secular purpose. The important question is whether these purposes can be met. Without a mind that is flexible, free and wise, you will fail to achieve either mundane or spiritual success in this world.

How do you go about the pursuit of happiness? As long as you insist, erroneously, that no one wants to have anything to do with you, it will not be possible to pursue happiness. For example, imagine there is a person sitting next to you, and that the person is an exact clone of yourself. Ask yourself whether you are willing to live with that person for the rest of your life. If the answer is no, then no one else can live with you either. How can you use your current personality and state of mind to create your own Pure Land? You need to replace your personality and mentality with a mind that is flexible, kind and wise. This should be the purpose of your life and cultivation.

The purpose of cultivation is to know how to live, and the purpose of life is to cultivate ourselves so that we can lead a life of happiness and peace. Poor relationships and a stagnant life cannot be dismissed as irrelevant to spiritual practice. One practitioner consulted me on a business matter: He wondered if, according to Buddhist teachings, it should matter if his business were successful or not. Should he simply be happy when business is good but not care so much when it is bad? This approach may seem right, but in truth it is fundamentally flawed. Business failure indicates inadequate mind capacity, wisdom and effort, just as it indicates that relationships and merits are less than ideal. When you are trapped in your own pattern of thinking, what you believed to be right is still wrong.

The meaning of life, when considered proactively, depends on whether you can transcend your limitations and establish a new reality. You may keep telling yourself that it does not matter how your business does, but in that case you are merely comforting yourself despite being locked within a prison of erroneous thinking. Most people lock themselves into self-made prisons of aimless, endless drifting. From that perspective, whether your business succeeds or not, it is all due to your attachments because you have not opened up to a new reality.

You must practice opening up the mind, dissolving limitations and manifesting a new reality in order to change your karma and be elevated. If you cannot do this, worldly happiness and spiritual growth will remain beyond your grasp. The mind can manifest everything, so why are you trapped in the phenomena you have created? You are trapped because the mind has attachments. Affliction begets affliction, fear creates fear, and issues in the mind will create more problems. The key is whether or not the mind can be its own master, open up a new reality and break through its self-made prison.

Ask yourself a question: What is your purpose in life? If your purpose is love and you accomplish it, then that is cultivation. If your purpose is happiness and you are able to accomplish it, then that is the reality you have opened up for yourself. It means you can harness the mind's power to achieve your purpose. If your goal is joy and you accomplish it, then you have mastered your mind and its creative power.

If you have failed to reach your goal, it means you are unfamiliar with your mind's creative power and do not know how to turn your thoughts around. You do not know how to use your mind. It means you have too many stubborn ideas, emotions and afflictions. When you are in this delusional state of mind, your wish for a wonderful future will remain only a self-deception. Thus there is really just one problem: Your mind cannot create what you want because you lack a malleable, lively, gentle and compassionate mind. You have no true understanding of your own creative power and are unable to let go of attachments.

Many people believe they should work hard to earn more money and make their families happy. Go ahead and give it a try. The question to ask, however, is whether you can really make it happen. With a state of mind that manifests the baggage of ego, worry, interpersonal disputes and self-centered opinions, can anyone really accomplish such a goal? Basically, it comes to this: Cultivation is life, and life is cultivation. To live a good life requires that you overcome your predicament. The same is true of cultivation. You must break free from your attachments. If you fail to break those attachments, you will suffer even as you struggle to move forward or retreat. Most people are stuck this way. They are vexed either going forward or turning back, and as a result they cannot break free from the confines of their situations.

Put Down the Baggage in Your Mind

The less baggage your mind bears, the better the phenomena it will create. The core of any problem is not in your current situation, it is in your state of mind. In other words, the problem is rooted in the idea and understanding within your mind. If your goal is to take care of your family and make sure everyone is happy, but in reality your family life is full of conflicts and problems, it is time to consider the matter of how to create what you want. The Mind's principle of creative power and ability remains the same whether you want to create happiness in life or to elevate yourself spiritually.

Consequently, a problem is never about others. Always ask yourself what ideas and personality flaws must be amended. The Mind already possesses an infinite capacity to create. There is no need to carry your fears, afflictions and attachments as you endeavor to manifest a favorable reality. It would be extremely challenging to hike to the peak of a mountain carrying the baggage of fear, worry, disputes and erroneous beliefs. Only after you set down your baggage can the goal be reached. What is here is already here. The important thing is to make your mind clear so that you know how to create your reality in the next moment.

The Mind is originally free and lively. It is we who have unnecessarily burdened the mind with garbage. If there is no improvement in your career, health and life, it means the mind cannot open up a new reality for you. Therefore, your self-made pattern of thinking has restricted you and propagated a number of issues.

Each of us has a mind that is originally free and at ease with itself. Anyone's mind can create desirable outcomes. This is the same for spiritual practice and worldly affairs. The stagnation of life and its outcome shows an inability to use the mind's creative power. You are the creator of your karma, so you can create either health and happiness or misery and erroneous beliefs.

Cultivation is the process of becoming the master of your thoughts, mind and reality. If you can free yourself from the tangle of attachments, you can break the impasse and establish a new reality in life. You must encourage yourself to be responsible. The past is already the past. You are exactly what you are right now. Your reality is already manifested as it is now. It is useless to obsess over it. Obsessive thoughts are simply baggage: They hold you back, and consequently you are unable to reach the peak. Set down that baggage so that you can reach the mountaintop.

A saying is often repeated in Buddhist temples: A true practitioner does not hold a grudge overnight. In other words, the

Mind is originally free, and its emptiness holds infinite possibilities. An overnight grudge is merely old baggage, so instead ask why you have created all that pain and frustration. Stop churning out miseries, and the miseries will cease to exist. Once you understand the idea, you can take up the responsibility of creating a better reality, and you will move toward the future you desire. This is true in spiritual cultivation and daily life.

Cultivation is mind dharma, and life is mind dharma. If you master the mind dharma, then everything will be in your possession. The person who opens a path toward spiritual enlightenment must also know how to achieve worldly happiness and love. A mind that is preoccupied by thought cannot create, no matter how much one might want to do so. The ancient saints said, "Buddha gains Nirvana through the Mind; such a mind is pure, calm and flawless." All Buddhas are freed through the Mind, which is pure, immaculate and able to manifest the desired phenomena.

Embroidered flowers look pretty but want fragrance;
Painted water, however wavy, attracts no fish.
Turning away from the wooden gate, beyond the little bridge;
Under the moon in the vast field, fish and flowers frolic.

6 THE LIMITLESS
CREATIVITY OF LIFE

Treasures hidden in Gold Mountain attract busy diggers;

No one can resist the metal-melting power

of widespread rumors.

To reach the goal, the entire family uprooted;

Misled route was marked with hearsay.

Homesick, one looks up longingly at the moon

shining over his hometown;

He dies an outsider in a strange land,

leaving loved ones far and behind.

It relies on the filial piety of their descendants

To guide these lost souls back home.

Mind Is the Source

The essence of Zen is liberation, freedom, creation and wisdom. You can perceive Zen as a wisdom that explores the nature of life. However, to live in harmony with the nature of life, you must first understand it. To avoid erroneous beliefs regarding Buddha, Zen Buddhism uses the term "Mind" and teaches that everyone must illuminate the Mind, calm the Mind and enlighten the Mind.

Zen Buddhism teaches that Mind is Buddha. While this clearly points out the goal of cultivation—the Buddha Mind—it is next to impossible to think that an individual's mind is the Buddha. Influenced by Buddhist teachings, people believe they are simply common beings with a huge distance between them and Buddha. They tend to focus on the idea of delusion, attachment and vexation, or the various sufferings and the karma of human life. These ideas become the focal point in the mind and leave less room for acceptance of the concept that Mind is Buddha.

Confidence in the teaching is like the roots of a tree: When the roots of confidence are shallow, blowing wind and flowing water—the external influences we experience—can cause the tree to fall. For instance, you might hear that the Mind is Buddha, but when you are out in public one curious glance from someone can make you completely forget the fact that the Mind is what gives rise to all phenomena. Instead, you begin to experience vexation and discomfort. This shows that your confidence in the teaching is not rooted deeply. A tree extends its roots deep down in one spot, and therefore a person should develop his or her faith upon one fundamental principle. That principle is that all phenomena are inseparable from the Mind and the Mind is Buddha.

If you recite the Diamond Sutra today, the Fahua Sutra tomorrow and the Amitabha Sutra the day after tomorrow, the roots of your confidence in the teaching will spread wide but will not deepen. A deep root develops through the right understanding, without which one cannot break free of the cycle of suffering until it is too late. If you waste your time fishing around for different ideas, when you encounter real-life situations none of the learning will be of much use. Many a long-time Buddhist cannot even remember the basic Buddhist teaching in the face of difficult situations because his understanding is not deep. Thus he is unable to handle the challenge he has encountered.

Western civilizations are dominated by the concept of God as the Creator; the maker of man. Contrastingly, the concept that all beings have Buddha nature is prevalent in Eastern thinking. Moreover, Confucian beliefs have been dominant in Chinese civilization for thousands of years. These concepts, Western and Eastern, act as the axis of culture, ideology and inheritance in their respective realms. One cannot discuss Chinese culture without referring to Confucius and Mencius; neither can one discuss American society without Christianity, or Europe and Latin America without Catholicism, or any Buddhist society without referring to Buddha. Ideological axes determine national culture.

The core of Zen Buddhism is the concept that Mind is the origin of life and everything else. Therefore, life without the Mind is like a piece of wood or a rock. Without you, there is no universe; your universe and everything in it exists because your mind exists. When you cease to exist, how is it even possible to conceive of the existence of others? Your universe includes your thoughts, your physical being and its environment, and the world you can see, no matter how far and wide. These are all creations of the Mind. Su Dongpo said, "The sound of a creek is no less than Buddha's tongue; the color of mountains is none other than the Buddha's pure body." Mountains, rivers and great landforms all exist as manifestations of the Mind.

Su Dongpo also said, "The void embodies everything; flowers, moon and pavilion." The Mind is formless and shapeless, but it reflects all. Only the formless can create forms; nothing with form can create another form. For example, the book in your hand cannot create another one. Everything with shape and form belongs to this world and is limited by time and space. That which is truly alive is shapeless and formless. It takes on various appearances in accordance with conditions, time and space.

You are wherever your mind is, as is your universe. Without the Mind, all phenomena such as your emotions, favorable circumstances and challenging predicaments are gone. Relatively undesirable appearances are called bad karma, and relatively desirable appearances are called good karma. Karma, however, is neutral. It is neither good nor bad.

Zen Buddhism brings Buddha from faraway India and directly into your mind. You must trust your mind, because the search for truth outside the Mind indicates a lack of responsibility for yourself. The Buddha statue in a temple is not there to demand lowly beings to bow but to dispel their stubborn illusions so they can see that Mind is Buddha. Thoughts and actions all arise from the Buddha Mind, and therefore we must return all thoughts and actions to our inner Buddha. The Buddha statue represents the essence of the Mind. Our body and ideas are functions of the Mind, and therefore the purpose of paying respect is to return to the essence of the Mind. The point is not to bow to a statue due to an externally seeking mindset but instead to reflect on the true Buddha within.

Why do we call Sakyamuni Buddha the "Fundamental Teacher?" This moniker refers to the Original Mind, which is our real Fundamental Teacher. A person who does not realize that Mind is Buddha would be taken in by various erroneous explanations of life's appearances and issues. Often a spiritual practitioner will blame ineffective cultivation on the assumption that his or her karma being is too strong. However, such an explanation of reality is never beneficial.

A Man of No Position Creates a Mundane World

The Mind creates all appearances and all existence. The fact that there are seven billion people in this world shows that the Mind has the ability to create seven billion different phenomena. The nature of the mind is the same for all people; everyone creates the reality of his life with this same basic nature of the Mind. Each person generates countless thoughts and situations from morning until night, from childhood until old age. Consider the innumerable personalities in our society. Are they not all manifestations of the Mind's creative power?

Buddhism refers to the mundane world in which we live as the "red dust" world. "Red" describes and represents attractiveness; "dust" symbolizes the phenomenon that comes and goes. Many attractive things come and go in this world, but in the end they must all be left behind. Most people react to the beautiful and pleasant with love and care but respond to the unpleasant with resistance, so they never accept life in its totality. Thus they cut up their lives into desirable red dust and undesirable gray dust. But all the dust is theirs, or it would not appear in their lives.

Zen Master Lin Ji taught his followers to look for this "true man of no position." Everything comes and goes like dust. Thoughts come, drop onto the floor like dust and disappear. One's body is like dust, as is his worldly appearance and even his life. All this dust is the phenomena created by the Mind. From Buddha and Boddhisatvas to hell, hungry ghosts and animals, everything is dust. So are our ideas, professions and the distinctions between rich and poor. Without dust there is neither manifestation nor a world.

The goal of cultivation is not to eliminate all dust. To do so would render life utterly lifeless. Buddha, relying on his formless body and mind, emerges in different worlds to help all beings. Buddha Mind has infinite creative power and is therefore capable of infinite manifestations in order to help beings in infinite forms of existence. Buddha is the most proactive creator of dust. When a person's mind is free from all limitations, he can elevate this creative capacity. An ordinary mind, however, becomes attached to the dust it has created. It restricts the original creativity of the Mind and lacks the ability to be free.

We have past, present, future and the phenomenal realms that pervade the ten directions. This shows that the Mind possesses infinite creative power. Out of attachment, the mind creates a particular appearance, which in turn limits its creative freedom. On the basis of this limiting reality, the mind continues the same pattern and creates similar appearances. Such a mind is not free. The continuous creation of similar things or experiences is called transmigration or, in Buddhism, *samsara*. However, the existence of *samsara* also demonstrates the Mind's creative capacity, because a dead mind cannot go through *samsara*. All suffering is created by a mind with attachments and delusions. The clear mind that is free of delusion can manifest as limitlessly as Buddha and Bodhisattvas to liberate all beings. However, an unclear mind that is misled by attachments creates dust of appearances, which transmigrate endlessly.

The Mind is vast as a void. It is ego-free but constantly energetic and powerful. To be free means to break away from the attachment to red dust. Buddhist teaching calls it guest dust, meaning that a visiting guest is bound to leave just as dust will fall to the ground. Accordingly, the function that arises from the Mind always goes away. To live a better life, it is critical that one find the source of all functions, which is the Mind.

Buddhist teaching distinguishes between the mundane and the transcendent. The mundane world consists of red dust in time and space, but the transcendent world refers to the source of all; to the true face of the Mind. An individual's thoughts and body result from the functions of his mind. Those functions, like dust, come and go. One should not deny the significance of dust because dust is existence; but dust will come and go like a guest. It is through the coming-and -going dust of the six senses that "a true man of no position" radiates his light and shakes the earth. This true man is the Mind, which is formless but able to function through various means.

Your Own Beliefs Are Not Reliable

Master Lang Ya, of the Song Dynasty, taught his disciples to inquire into this "true man of no position." At the time, there was an old woman called Granny Yu who sold fried sweet rice cake for a living. One day she came to ask Master Lang Ya whether she too could study Zen. "Of course," said Lang Ya. Zen Buddhism simply teaches you to discover your mind, and it reveals your mind. The mind can generate thoughts. Poor thoughts will lead to trouble in your physical body, personality and relationships with others. It is necessary to learn how to use the mind skillfully in order to attain a better life. If you do not, you will suffer.

A disciple once asked me how to go about establishing positive thinking. I told him that positive thinking is not a choice but a necessity. It is worth noting that the desire for the positive is actually built on a foundation of negativity, in which one is trying to migrate from the negative to the positive. Therefore, while this type of positive thinking appears to be positive, it is actually just another form of negative thinking. For example, many people shop at the organic food markets, wanting to eat healthy food. However, is this desire for health really positive? Often, a fear of illness is the real motivation. Thus the way to truly establish positive thinking is a very subtle, delicate matter because what appears to be positive is not always positive in nature. True, positive thinking is not based on duality, and thinking that arises without attachment is truly positive.

Why do you want to do more meditation? It could be that you are afraid your teacher will check on you. Why do you work so hard on your cultivation? It could be driven by your fear of death and transmigration or by your desire to be free from suffering. If so, you are not necessarily being truthful and responsible for yourself. How do you expect to part from suffering if you do not realize that you have created the suffering? Be careful not to be deceived by your seemingly positive thinking. A person may become ill despite a diet of organic foods. Cultivation based on fear is not an act of taking responsibility because you are avoiding the attachments underneath the fear. Instead, you must face yourself and your responsibility in cultivation. Do not rely entirely on a positive thinking model, which is just another way to avoid reality.

People, when faced with certain situations, habitually think that their opinion or approach regarding the situation is right. But often they do not know why they fundamentally believe their own assessments. Think about it: You might firmly believe that you are right, but at the same time this self-righteousness causes frustration and hardship. Now, in a similar pattern you are trying to establish positive thinking, assuming that it will be helpful. But is that not just another way of deceiving yourself? How much real progress can be made by trying to build a positive life within the same mental framework that created all the problems in the first place?

Generally, a person cannot realize his real belief, but enlightenment is assured if someone really understands the true self. People, however, are normally at a loss as to where their thoughts come from, how the principle of causality operates in the mind and how the mind functions. Here is a simple way to test how your mind actually operates: Simply look at your relationships, your appearance, your body and the situations that surround you. You can get a sense of how your life is operating. The Mind is very cunning and elusive, but the appearances it creates are telling. Various issues in your life are indications of deviation from the functioning of the Mind. The thought process you believe to be correct is not working, so adjustment is required.

The Mind's creation is real, but what people believe—their definition of reality—is largely false. The question is whether or not you can see through the deception and let go. You might tell someone who has lost a son that it is his karma to have experienced such a loss, but would you accept such karma if the same thing happened to you? Man has many answers to his questions, but none of them can solve the real problems. However, he will give these useless answers as advice to others. The reason we cannot make progress in life is because we continue to deceive ourselves. Regardless of how you explain it, your way of interacting with others, all your learning and efforts, and your justified behaviors and opinions can only make you what you are right now. Therefore, even if you cannot penetrate your true thoughts, you should at least see the consequences they cause.

It is never easy, of course, to build truly positive thinking within habitual thinking and frame of mind. Consider the person who is critical, argumentative and fond of politics. While studying Buddhism, he may avoid debating others about politics, but he is most likely to start arguing with others about Buddhist philosophy because his argumentative personality has not changed. It takes self-awareness to dismantle the old frame of mind and build a new one.

People often talk about "awareness" in the West, by which they mean a kind of wakefulness. True awareness, however, does not come easily. It comes from a pure, free, active mind that has perfected its creativity. Contrastingly, the so-called consciousness and subconsciousness are all delusions, lacking clarity. Sometimes I ask my students whether they feel clear-minded at the moment. Some say yes, but others say no. No matter what state you are in right now, have you ever experienced more clarity than right now? Of course you have! If so, then your present state of clear-mindedness is still, by contrast, not clear. Clarity is relative.

Ask yourself whether your motivation for an action is truly positive or whether you are acting merely out of fear or hunger for power. Often, what propels a person's life is not what he superficially considers right or positive. The truth is often just the opposite, because such a life is based on fear. Know the true basis of your thoughts, because they run your life. The thoughts that appear on the surface of the mind are merely disguises.

Deceived by your own erroneous beliefs, you may lose faith and hope. You might see this world as flawed and unfair: *I work so hard, so why do things end up like this for me?* If this happens, it is because you do not understand the true basis of your thoughts. As the Buddhist teaching puts it, "Be careful not to trust your own beliefs, because they are not reliable." Even though you may not yet know your true self, at least you can evaluate how your mind functions by looking at the results, meaning whether you have become more compassionate and wise or if your relationships have improved.

Break Old Habits and Explore New Paths

A person once came to me to ask for a second opinion regarding a certain matter. He wanted to hear another's opinion and consider different thoughts and perspectives. I told him that it is impossible for one mind to hold a second opinion. Some people say they are very objective, but if this objectivity comes from their perspective, what difference does it make if they are being objective or subjective? How can one really be objective? When you are in a bad mood, try to calm your mind and you will feel like a different person. Your thoughts will no longer be the disturbing viewpoints of one who is upset.

Any thought that comes from a disturbed mind will stray from reality. Once calmed, however, the perspective and scope of the person's viewpoint will change and he or she can see more clearly. Such a state, however, is not perfect clarity. To see everything with perfect clarity, the ego must go so that there is no grasping of self-created phenomena. As long as there is an ego, the degree of freedom and initiative of the mind's creativity will be limited to certain directions.

The creativity and flexibility of the Mind is therefore limited if it can only function in a fixed direction. Therefore, the only way to increase the creativity and liveliness of the Mind is to deconstruct that direction. To function according to one's ego attachment is similar to driving along a single road: There is no way to branch off in various directions. Many a person will strive to build a positive frame of mind, but very few actually have a life of positivity because they do not know where they are right now. Your life is based upon your self-perception, and consequently the selfless mind must function through your inner ego attachment. It is difficult to take responsibility for who you think you are, because you can easily be deceived if you do not clearly perceive the foundation of your thoughts.

Let us revisit the story of Granny Yu. Having visited Master Lang Ya, Granny Yu went about her life selling rice cakes and pondering the phrase, "true man of no position." One day she overheard a beggar singing, "Were it not for Liu Yi's letter, how could I ever return to Tongting Lake?" Granny Yu came to enlightenment at once and went to Master Lang Ya for his confirmation. Lang Ya asked her to describe the "true man of no position," and she replied with this verse:

Here is a man of no position, with three heads, six arms and huge eyes staring hard; one strike of his arm, Mount Hua divides into two, and ten-thousand years of flowing never knew the spring.

The "true man" is ever-changing and omnipresent: joy, anger, sadness and happiness are his own making. The formless mind projects thousands of appearances, as in the phrase "six arms, three heads and big eyes staring." Once Mount Hua splits—meaning that man's attachment to duality is shattered—ten thousand years of flowing water knows not the spring. The myriad creations of the Mind—past, present and future, social status and responsibility—are all like flowing water. They are simply dust. Without attachment, one can create and use the dust freely. If you still think you are angry, it is no longer the timeless, flowing water. Anger is optional. It is not the fundamental Mind that can create all.

The purpose of studying Zen is to know your mind as well as your life. It is not an outward pursuit but is instead an inner discipline that provides you with the ability to abide in the nature of the Mind and dissolve attachments. It is the process of dismantling the erroneous belief system that resides in your mind. Therefore, Zen masters often negate everything. For example, Master Gui Shan asked Xiang Yan, "What was it like before you were born to your parents?" No matter what Xiang Yan answered, Gui Shan shook his head. What anyone deems right or wrong—and even an individual's self-perception—is the result of attachment. We should practice restraining the ego.

Do many of your past beliefs need revision today? How many of your beliefs today will need adjustment in the future? If so, why must you hold onto those beliefs so firmly? They are a waste of energy and will only lead to more problems. Spend your effort on breaking your ego attachments, and you will free the infinitely creative Mind.

Do not be fooled by your own thoughts. Do not drive along the same old road. Instead, retrain your mind in order to know the foundation of your thoughts in their various appearances. Break down the attachment within your mind. Once your mind is restored to its primordial, formless nature, it becomes perfected, encompassing the entirety of the ten directions and possessing the utmost creativity. To liberate your mind, you must face your true self. Cultivation is neither cosmetic nor superficial, it is knowing your own mind. Know your mind, and you will know Zen and your life. By knowing your life, you can experience limitless creativity.

I have a riddle for you to puzzle over;
It is neither the elephant's trunk nor its chin.
Originally it is pitch-dark and invisible;
Lamps break, riddle solved, and light shines.

7 THE TRUE SIGNIFICANCE OF CULTIVATION

The Eight Immortals across the ocean display their magic;
In and out of clouds they transform so easily.
One imperial edict from the Jade Emperor
brought them back to the Golden Palace;
There they serve His Majesty for imperial rewards.

Before Cultivation, Identify the Main Goal

Spiritual cultivation can be monotonous, and monotony may seem boring and lonely to people who live fast-paced lives. Cultivation, however, calms the Mind and generates mental clarity and purity. Busy people, lacking the ability to appreciate this happiness of mental clarity, interpret spiritual cultivation as being dull and listless. The truth is that a calm mind has the greatest creative potential. It can generate a long-lasting joy that is not dependent on any external stimulation. Nevertheless, before one can reach that state of mind, one must undergo a process of physical and spiritual cleansing and a long period of training.

Whether you recite Buddha's name or engage in Zen inquiry, cultivation means the strengthening of your focus by doing the same thing day in and day out. It could be meditating on a *hua tou* or a question word. Regardless of the result, the meditation continues every day. After five, ten or twenty years, the desired outcome will eventually occur. The process of cultivating the mind is simple and ordinary; it should never be one method today and another method tomorrow. A restless mind finds it difficult to focus, but the depth and breadth of knowledge can only be attained through a prolonged, focused effort. Aimless practice achieves little.

Cultivation must be based on the core principle that each of us is our own creator and that the Mind creates all appearances, which manifest instantaneously in response to the Mind's functioning. Anchoring your practice to this principle—returning all phenomena and ideas to this central concept—is the training of Mind dharma. It is time-consuming, because people are deeply accustomed to the dualistic notion of seeking reality outside the Mind. It takes a long time simply to replace the thoughts that have both positive and negative aspects with those that are pure goodness. If you do not do this, you will suffer endlessly. It takes both time and wise discipline to clear out the old, bring in the new and transform your beliefs.

A viable method of cultivation requires that deluded, erroneous ideas must first be replaced with the right view of reality. People tend to lose patience, however, because they are not aware that this is necessary. Cultivation requires commitment in order that the mind can become settled and acquire the ability to focus. If one lacks the right understanding, concerted practice of more than five, ten or even twenty years will only lead to further deviation. Any effort that does not support the goal of moving toward the true meaning of life will be futile.

Spiritual cultivation requires that you restrain your behavior. If you tend to rush at everything, try doing things slowly and mindfully. This is an act of restraint. Avoid being overly chatty, because gossiping is a self-indulgent, phenomena-grasping behavior. Do not underestimate these small things, however. It would be an accomplishment of a lifetime if you could simply end the habit of gossiping. As an ancient saying puts it, "Over-competitiveness brings frustration; wordiness ends in disputes."

The restraint of behavior does not mean burying your feelings. For example, it is wrong to hold a grudge, even if you do not mouth a single word against others. However, if you trick yourself into thinking your gossip is simply words that do not represent your mind, you will unconsciously fall into the habitual tendencies of a gossip. Cultivation and daily life, like a carriage drawn by two horses going in opposite directions, become divorced from each other when people do not know how to correctly practice restraint.

A confused, fragmented understanding inevitably leads to confused, fragmented cultivation. Therefore, you should first be clear in your understanding before any progress can be expected through practice. It is a process of moving toward a single point, a single truth. Theravada Buddhism teaches the cultivation of morality, concentration and wisdom. Cultivation, in our context, means correction and restraint with focus on the ability to direct one's thought. Without morality and concentration, wisdom cannot manifest itself.

Wisdom is an innate virtue of the Mind. Upon enlightenment, the fundamental wisdom is attained as it arises from the absence of ego. Then, through further cultivation you gain the acquired wisdom that can give rise to an infinite variety of functions. However, fundamental wisdom alone does not ensure that you will be able to reveal the complete virtue of the Mind. Once fundamental wisdom is gained, you must eliminate all erroneous beliefs and attachments and thereby reveal the complete virtue of the Mind. Accordingly, in the Three Refuge vows we say, "I shall take refuge in the dharma; may all beings delve deeply into the treasury of teaching, possessing wisdom as vast as the ocean." It is the essence of wisdom to penetrate the causal source of phenomena—the Mind as the vehicle and the creator of all phenomena—and remain fully awake in the Mind's function.

The virtue of the Mind will show itself as long as your vexations and attachments are broken down, restrained and pacified. You employ moral disciplines to subdue external habits and attachments, and you use singular focus of the mind to subdue your inner habits and attachments. After severing your external and internal grasping, wisdom will then be manifested. For example, a practical approach to mind training is to keep your eyes and ears shut so you can subdue your inner disturbances by focusing on a single point. Your life will benefit from the ability to voluntarily withdraw yourself from your mental habits. This kind of focused withdrawal is a constructive practice method.

The reason the mind is not in charge of itself is because we lack the strength to restrain our mental habits. Therefore, we react to pleasurable and unpleasant conditions, giving rise to all kinds of thoughts. Indeed, the mind will wander all over. The key to practice is to bring the mind under our control so that we can act properly, and as a result the mind will gradually regain control of itself.

Mahayana Buddhism teaches the six perfections, or the six pure practices of the Bodhisattvas: generosity, morality, forbearance, effort, concentration and wisdom. The practice of a Bodhisattva is not a lack of focus. Instead, it is aimed at a wider scale of letting go and practicing more comprehensive self-restraint, but it has the same ultimate goal of uncovering the Buddha nature. The pure practices of the Bodhisattvas focus on controlling the tendency to seek truth outside the Mind.

Generosity, in specific terms, subdues greed. Morality subdues illicit behaviors. Forbearance subdues negative karma, even when we encounter troubling situations that arise from our personality flaws. Because each of us is the creator of his or her own problems, one is actually practicing the patient forbearance of oneself, not forbearance of the external world. Effort subdues the chaos of the mind caused by mental lethargy and delusion. That mental chaos is what prevents us from applying the right understanding so as to achieve a wholesome life, since effort is essentially an act of restraint. Concentration subdues confusion and leads to wisdom. Thus the path of the Bodhisattva is more comprehensive. It provides more skillful means for practicing restraint. Each method of restraint serves as an antidote to false views and actions, which would otherwise seek truth outside the Mind.

We often hear the saying, "Before reaching Buddhahood, one should first form good human relationships." If the purpose of creating good relationships is not Buddhahood, then fostering good will with one another is simply a form of seeking truth outside the Mind. Most people create many relationships but never make it to Buddhahood. Instead, they build up many good and bad relationships, mistake them as the goal of the Bodhisattva practice and end up letting the mind degenerate. The path to Buddhahood is a process of restraint, which is implemented through a variety of skillful means. Do not mistake the compassion and extensiveness of the six Bodhisattva practices as permission to run loose without discipline. Without restraint, it will be very difficult to engage in a spiritual practice.

To Subdue the Bandits, You Must Capture the Leader

All Buddhist sects—Mahayana, Theravada and the Esoteric—and their teachings are intended for human cultivation. Every human being, whether rich or poor, has greed, anger, delusion, pride and skeptical doubt. These traits are fundamental to our human nature. Our lives and phenomenal realities share many more similarities than differences. As human beings, we are neither heavenly beings nor beasts, and we are generally the same in terms of physical appearance, our likes, dislikes and our tendencies, whether wholesome or destructive. As human beings, we share a strong tendency to seek the truth outside the Mind. We have the kinds of thoughts that are unique to human beings and the corresponding karma. As the Mind functions differently, different patterns of life emerge.

The elevation of the mind requires that one gradually withdraw from seeking the truth outside the mind so that the source of life can be recognized. This process of withdrawal must be supported by the right view. The purpose of various spiritual philosophies and practices is to eliminate an erroneous understanding of life. If Theravada does not cut off the tendency to grasp at phenomenal conditions, Mahayana does not lead to the realization that all beings possess the Buddha Nature and Esoteric Buddhism does not lead one to realize the essence of Mind, then each of them will miss the point.

Many Buddhist groups today hope to spread spiritual teachings throughout the world. It is essential that the teachings they spread are universally true, without exception. The Christian concept that faith in God guarantees eternity is not a universal principle, because it only saves those who have faith. Even though the concept that "God loves the world" is universal, do the churches and institutions that support this concept practice it in reality as well as in theory? God in this understanding is neither Christian nor Islamic but is instead universal. However, if the love applies to those who believe in the concept but not for those who do not, the teaching of such love will lack relevance.

The Buddhist principle that all beings have Buddha nature is true whether or not you believe in it. If you do not believe in this concept, you still possess the Buddha nature. Therefore, the concept is universally applicable, and all cultivation and practice must be anchored to it. Although specific methods such as meditation, chanting mantra or sutra, or reciting Buddha's name differ from region to region and are not universal, they share the universal goal of restraining and withdrawing the mind from its tendency to seek truth outside. They deliver the practitioner to the ultimate truth, not unlike the way in which Christianity delivers its followers back to God. Regardless of your religious affiliation, the practice of withdrawal based on the highest truth is universal.

Occasionally someone will ask me about the rules of meditation, and I give this reply: As long as a method can help you focus and stay away from erroneous thoughts, it is considered helpful. Is the

Christian prayer practice beneficial? Yes, of course it is. With palms pressed together in sincerity, Christian prayers can help the mind find calmness. If you can paint a talisman, worship Confucius or Lao Tzu or even prostrate to a rock with focus of mind, that focused mind will produce a corresponding effect. This is universally true. It is not strictly necessary to perform seated meditation in order to calm the mind. Different methods have different levels of depth and potency, but all are useful in your cultivation as long as they serve to restrain the mind.

Buddhist teaching, as it is based on a principle that is beneficial and universally true, has neither issues nor limitations in regard to geography, religion, culture, race or human affairs. Only such a universal principle is capable of benefiting all beings. Therefore, cultivation must be practical and relevant to our reality. Setting aside religion for a moment, what can we accomplish in this world in our present reality as human beings? As human beings we must live with the reality of an ever-changing world, as our opinions, physical bodies and the environment are constantly evolving. Because we cannot escape change but can only do so for the better or the worse, we must learn to live with change and make the best use of it.

Impermanence remains the truth, whether you believe in God, Buddha or Allah. Thus the purpose of faith is to elevate the individual within this constantly changing world. You learn to love, have faith and be a better person, and gradually you are changed for the better. It is an evolutionary process whereby a person is at first non-believing, then believing but not practicing and then practicing with complete faith. This process is widely accepted, and it applies to all religions.

The religions of the East and West, as well as the various Buddhist sects, have distinctive origins due to their unique geographies, histories, social structures and cultures. No matter how widespread one particular tradition becomes, there will inevitably be non-believers. No tradition can transcend its inherent limitations. However, it is clear that because the Mind is the source of all phenomena, all vexations can be resolved when one properly restrains the mind. As it is said, "To subdue the bandits, you must capture their leader first," and in this case the leader is none other than the Mind. To rest in the nature of Mind is to find the source. Even religions and their various sects originate from the root of life, which is the Mind. Through the principle of the Mind, we can handle life's myriad manifestations.

Master Yen Yang paid a visit to Master Zhao Zhou one day. Yen Yang asked, "What happens when there is nothing left?" In reply, Zhao Zhou said, "Put it down." Yen Yang asked, "But there is nothing. What do I put down?" Zhao Zhou then said, "Then take it up." This seems like a very Zen-ish dialogue, or a philosophical one. When there is nothing left, it is similar to when one inquires deeply into the nature of the self and reaches the very beginning: the root of life. At that point one simply rests there and lives with the realization of the source at all times. The question is thus: Are you able to escape change? Can you ever escape the capacity of the Mind to create? No, that is impossible. Since you cannot, you must either pick it up or take on this truth.

You must learn how to create, how to generate thoughts, and how to manifest your reality from the Mind in order to live a life that is truly joyful. The moment you function with the Mind is nothing but emptiness, and consequently you never grasp the Mind's creation. To create without grasping is the way to manifest perfection and harmony while being liberated within it.

A Fundamental Understanding of the Nature of the Mind Can Dissolve Disputes

Each of us has individual beliefs. We define the external world with our own beliefs and interact with our own definition of the world. Such definitions are our prison: We cannot escape those definitions unless we destroy the prison. It is possible to destroy certain prisons, but there are other kinds of prisons that cannot be broken, such as the prison of impermanence and the prison of the cause and result of the Mind's functioning. Since these latter prisons cannot be destroyed, you must learn how to live with them and make good use of them. Because you cannot change the Mind's capacity to generate thoughts and functions, instead you must practice how to generate thoughts and functions that are beneficial to yourself and others.

If you cannot live outside of a principle, it is universal regardless of your religious belief. Theravada, Mahayana and the Esoteric sect have distinct interpretations of Buddhist teachings, but those interpretations are simply the result of the karma of the followers, in which different karmas create different interpretations, teachings and ideas. People gather according to different karmas, and the individuals thus gathered, with their different karmas, share a common karma. That karma is, in turn, the collective manifestation of the group's life. Whether of an individual or a group, all phenomena are karma. It may be reasonable, to some degree, to deem one person's karma superior to another's, simply because the world is relative. However, every man's karma possesses positive and negative aspects. A universal principle transcends the dualities of good versus evil, pro and con and superiority versus inferiority.

You must learn and practice the universal truth in order to elevate your life. That is the goal of all cultivation. Outside the universal truth, there is nothing but relative truth deployed for the sake of convenience. These relative truths create nothing but dualistic confrontation. To know the universal truth, you must break the ties that bind you and break the attachment of the ego. Otherwise, you will be trapped in a delusion of your own making. When everyone holds onto his own belief as right, there is always conflict and argument. These beliefs are limiting because they are reflections of self-attachment.

Muslims, Christians and Buddhists all believe in the truths of their religions and lead their lives accordingly. Human beings, through their beliefs and actions, mold themselves into Muslims, Christians and Buddhists. Even the atheist who claims not to believe in anything still lives according to his or her atheistic beliefs and thereby creates a karmic reality.

The capacity of the Mind, however, transcends all religions and teachings. Only the Mind, with its endless wisdom and complete truth, is called Buddha. It sees truth as a whole; it does not seek truth from a limited perspective. Ask yourself whether what you see, study, practice and follow is the truth. If it cannot solve your problems or even enlighten you, then you must keep searching within. Only the universal truth can eradicate the habitual tendencies that create inner-outer conflicts and bring wholesomeness to your life. To mistake chanting and worshiping the Buddha statue for Buddhist cultivation is to seek truth outside the Mind. Only by understanding the nature of the Mind can one's cultivation become relevant to the reality.

Enlightenment is not possible without the guidance of the universal truth, which transcends any religion or individual. A dualistic concept, however conveniently followed, can only take you from one corner to another corner. It is not the ultimate answer but is in fact a source of controversy and dispute. From the ancient times until today, only those who have followed the universal truth have reached the Tao, to have their legacies widely witnessed and spread. Sakyamuni Buddha had 1,250 disciples who accompanied him at all times, and each and every one of them achieved enlightenment. Sakyamuni Buddha's teaching was the universal truth, and his disciples practiced accordingly.

The modern-day world has seen far fewer instances of spiritual realization because the principles people follow are not necessarily universal. Instead of following the universal truth, people tend to grasp the surface appearances of various Buddhist sects, such as Zen, Pure Land and others, and become perplexed. Despite their diligence, they remain ignorant of the universal truth. Neither their understanding nor their behavior is compatible with the universal truth. The result is that any wish they have to spread the teaching will fail. If a person's understanding is false, the capacity of the mind will be limited and vexations cannot be resolved.

All enlightened masters realize the nature of the Mind. This is true in the past and present, and it will be true in the future. The truth is the same whether it applies to ancient people or those of modern times, whether in the East or in the West. The Mind's original face is universal; it does not depend on our beliefs. The universal truth is like a huge cage from which no one—either a believer or a non-believer—can escape. All scriptures must be understood through the universal truth of the Mind, and all vexations must be dissolved through the universal truth of the Mind. Otherwise, inner conflict cannot be eliminated nor enlightenment attained.

Your ideas, being different from those of others, are by default not universal, but the ability of each person to have his own ideas is indeed universal. The Pure Land of the Medicine Buddha is naturally different from the Pure Land of Amitabha Buddha or Sakyamuni Buddha. Their separate realms, origins and appearances, however, have all attained the state of perfection of manifestation. Even the Buddha must hold fast to the Mind principle of dependent-origination, the principle "Mind is Buddha" and the principle of ever-changing phenomena. Through these universal principles, any religion or individual can attain enlightenment.

The universal truth defuses and dissolves conflicts among religions and disputes about right versus wrong and good versus evil, because it is applicable to all. This is what must be conveyed to everyone for understanding and realization. What the Buddha taught is a wisdom that requires time to understand through experience. Every step of practice takes us deeper into understanding the truth. Realization alone does not guarantee the ability to manifest reality accordingly; there is still some distance to travel along the path. The enlightened beings spent decades seeking the universal truth so that they could then master their own lives through this true principle. Apart from the universal truth, there is very little of what you know that can encourage the growth of your mind and spirit.

A caged parrot longs for the world outside;
Searching up and down, he sees no rift anywhere.
Day after day, his master opens the little door to feed him;
He has had to mimic his laugh and countenance.
Exhausted but with a full stomach,
He caters to visiting guests whenever they feel like some fun.
One day, he pecks open a rift and sees the vast universe;
Only then does it dawn on him how blind he has been.

8 RESTRAINT AND CREATION

In Mount Flower and Fruit lives the magical Monkey King;
He made such a scene in the Imperial Palace through
his countless transformations.
Although he managed to steal and eat the Peach of Immortality;
He still could find no way to escape from the Buddha's hand.

Problems Are Self-Created

Cultivation is a type of self-control that is used to draw back the thoughts and functions of the Mind. Many Zen masters devote themselves to one-year, ten-year and even twenty-year retreats in isolation, whereby they engage in the training process of control. Meditation is also a form of control. During meditation we withdraw the mental energy that would otherwise be invested in thoughts. When we encounter an emergency or difficulty and the mind becomes disturbed, self-control helps us to set our thinking aside so that the mind can stay calm. The process of self-control restores the mind to a tranquil state.

God is the source of all life in the West. In Zen, it is the Mind, which enables you to hear, see, think, feel, generate thoughts and change behavior. If you do not know the Mind, it means you do not know the source of your illness, afflictions and attachments. You can only have a single source of life. Otherwise, if there were two sources, you would be two individuals. If you do not know this singular source, you will have no orientation in life and will not be able to comprehend the reason for your state of reality.

Master Ling Mo became a monk under Master Ma Zu. One day, Ling Mo went to pay a visit to Master Shi Tou, saying, "If you say it right, I'll stay; if wrong, I'll leave." Master Shi Tou, taking no notice of what Ling Mo said, sat down in his usual place. Seeing this, Ling Mo decided to leave. Then he heard Master Shi Tou call out, "Monk." Ling Mo turned around, and Master Shi Tou continued, "From birth to death, it is just this. What do you turn around for?" Ling Mo was instantly enlightened.

"From birth to death, it is just this. What do you turn around for?" This *koan* illustrates that turning around is yet another result of the function of the Mind, as are behaviors, relationships and everything else. The manifestation of Mind is all-pervasive, and therefore even the changes in the landscape and the state of your health are functions of the Mind. You have thoughts, behaviors and the ability to create; therefore, you cannot escape from the world you have created. For example, if you study Confucianism and its principles of benevolence, righteousness, propriety, wisdom and integrity, those principles will be rooted in your mind. Your health, relationships and all other appearances will be created through these principles.

People in Christian or Islamic countries live with their God through channels that are formed by the teaching and principles of their religions. God represents eternal life, joy and freedom from suffering, and such rewards are the believer's life goals. Those religions teach believers to follow their religious principles in order to reach their goals.

The majority of our time on earth is, in reality, tied up in dealing with problems, diseases and difficulties. Suffering is not simply a Buddhist concept but is a universal problem. All people must face people. Most people's life ideals and goals are fragmented, and few of us can remain committed to our ideals and goals throughout our lives. It is said, "He who lacks long-standing plans is bound to encounter immediate troubles." However, the opposite is also true: A person who is surrounded by immediate troubles finds he cannot plan far ahead. Even if dreams exist, it is difficult to fulfill them.

If the immediate goals are to be happy, healthy and worry-free, Christians will turn to God because He is the Creator and Zen Buddhists will turn to the Mind because all forms are the Mind's creation. Even though mankind has manufactured airplanes and satellites, we remain ignorant of the fact that thoughts, bodies, relationships and environments are also man-made.

Prior to any discussion regarding a Buddhist's notion of Nirvana, Confucian saints or God, ask yourself whether you can handle your daily problems properly. Let us suppose you believe in God. You understand that eternal life and joy lie with God, but right at this moment do you feel even a tiny amount of joy? If not, you know there is quite a gap between you and God. Likewise, for most people Nirvana and sainthood are distant, but family issues, parenting problems and health concerns—which are again your own creations— are right in front of you. They should be taken care of, but you have a tough time handling them.

You may have already realized that the source of all issues is yourself, even if you are not fully aware of it. You do not simply run into predicaments, but instead your mind creates them due to delusion and continues to embrace them. Be sure, however, that there is no problem or issue unless you have created it.

Imagine that you are a television. The reason you see an image is because you, the television, are set to that particular channel. There are many channels in your mind, and whatever channel you tune into, the corresponding show will appear. Until an individual has fully internalized this notion, instead of practicing self-cultivation he will blame his problems on external conditions. If your problems were the result of external conditions, then the problems would dissipate if you could eliminate those conditions. Think about what your most recent problem is. It may have to do with your husband or wife, or perhaps an issue with your health or work. Does your trouble end if you simply get rid of the element you believe to have caused the problem? Without all the factors involved, certainly you will continue to have afflictions. Human beings find trouble by tuning to these channels and becoming obsessed with them. If you do not feel like crying, you will not cry. If you do not create difficulty, there will not be any. When all is said and done, it is really a single problem that afflicts the human species: They do not know how to create what they want using their own mind.

Self-Control Must Be Thorough and Complete

One should always try, when discussing a particular topic with a person, to understand that individual's state of mind as reflected in what he or she says instead of fixating on the other person's opinion. Similarly, I was once told that questions from the mentally ill should be handled very carefully. In that case, what truly matters is not how to answer the questions themselves but how to understand the unstable state of mind behind the question. If a person's mind is unstable, his or her questions are not likely to be based on reality. The reality, however, is that the mind is unstable. If you approach the questions from the surface level, how many questions can you handle if they keep bringing up questions? Can you handle them all? To a certain degree, each individual's mentality is somewhat flawed and blurred. These mental states—attachments—become the channel through which to manifest afflictions and pain. Therefore, it is most important to find out more about a person's attachment instead of simply dealing with an individual's phenomenon.

A clear mind knows how each issue comes about and what causes it. If you do not understand why you are facing a problem, such as an illness or a relationship issue, then you do not know where your mind is or how it manifests such phenomenon. It is difficult to manage the problem because your mind lacks clarity. The habit of blaming every problem on external conditions and pointing fingers at this person or that thing indicates a kind of split personality or a mental problem, in which one does not recognize the source of his or her problems and perceptions.

If your mind is not clear regarding how to resolve problems, they will manifest themselves repeatedly. However, an approach that focuses on the mind state goes to the root: Change the channel through which the mind functions and you will not give rise to the problem again. For instance, to change crying to laughter requires more than a change of facial expression. The mind must function differently and give rise to the thought of laughter.

The first step toward solving any problem is to acknowledge that you are the only one in the universe who ought to encounter this problem. Accept it willingly, and the mind will be calmed. Accept everything you encounter willingly, because it is a fact. It is not a matter of choice, since you are already involved in it. The search for answers outside yourself is like seeking truth outside the Mind. Nothing outside yourself can be the true cause, because the real question and answer are nothing but you.

An average person sees phenomena as separate from himself, but a person in cultivation sees them as part of himself. A Buddhist deals with appearances and problems through self-control. This is exemplified by the process of daily meditation in which he restrains the energy of the mind's functions, particularly those that, when misused, will result in all kinds of problems. Because suffering, afflictions and attachments are all creations of the mind, you should restrain the mind's creative power until you learn how to use it properly.

The practice of withdrawal involves restraint. It means pulling back the unskillful actions of the mind. With an awareness that the mind has created our trouble, we refrain from further creation and withdraw everything back to its origin, which is the Mind. Once we have returned to the true face of the Mind, we can create what we wanted from this standpoint. Back in the era of the Buddha, the material environment and human affairs were simpler and it was relatively easy to withdraw the mind. Modern people have much more material dependency, so the process of withdrawal is more complex.

The more dependent on appearances a person is, the more

limited his mind's creativity will be. Therefore, the best solution to all problems is self-restraint, because less dependency will lead the mind to greater creative power. Self-restraint through practices such as meditation will hold back the unskillful functions of the mind, diminishing disease, vexation, pain, attachment and delusion. Eventually, it will eliminate the ego attachment so that the mind no longer functions by seeking outside itself. At this stage, there is an end to all trouble and suffering.

Liberation is about shedding attachment so that the mind's creativity can be freed and come alive. True liberation comes when we are not attached to our self-created personalities and beliefs, and at that moment the mind attains absolute freedom. In the time of the historical Buddha, spiritual practice was very simple. It was not burdened with anything nonessential, and consequently people practiced by directly facing their problems. Once the practice of self-control is complete, liberation is obtained and every issue in life is resolved.

The Buddhist concept of liberation is essentially based on self-control. However, many Buddhist followers face a dilemma: Their heavy habits prevent them from achieving a complete withdrawal from the power that causes their problems, so they are stuck in the middle of the river, so to speak. They are neither able to reach "the other shore" nor can they return. While practicing self-control, some people mistakenly believe that any form of creativity is to be eliminated, so they suppress all forms of it. This situation can be compared to reining a horse so he cannot run wild but also limiting his ability to pull a cart. Similarly, sometimes a practitioner, during the process of self-restraint, will also diminish his own energy for the sake of wholesome karma.

You may practice very hard in regard to self-control, doing meditation, chanting and prayers, but does it solve the issues of real life? If not, then your mind is still engaged in a deluded mode of functioning. Many people, due to inadequate effort, limited time or insufficient understanding, find despite considerable effort that they cannot transform even simple habits, afflictions and attachments. Many people are stuck in this transitional period. Having practiced for some time, they find that they are less energetic, less active and quite passive.

The ancient Buddhists were much more resolute than are modern people in regard to enlightenment. They went directly toward the goal of enlightenment. Modern people, on the other hand, have relatively weak self-control. We vacillate in our afflictions but cannot move forward. Consider your own life. Are you proactive in creating and improving your own reality? For most of us, the answer is "No." We tend to say, "Do not fight for this, do not try that." The ancient practitioners, however, were very courageous and took responsibility for their thoughts and actions. Buddha Sakyamuni, for instance, once determined that he would not get up from his seat under the Bodhi tree until he was enlightened. Most modern people lack such courage and willingness to take responsibility. Therefore, despite daily meditation, they are still confused and lost, like lost souls wandering in the void between two lives.

Very few practitioners today can clearly conceptualize the end of birth and death, despite the need to do so. To end birth and death is to find your mind and know your mind, so that you can return to the original state of the Mind and make use of it skillfully. Modern people must model themselves after the ancient saints and cultivate with clear goals, responsibilities and focused efforts. Practice requires the right view. Do not see cultivation as too challenging. Do not wish for fast results or complain that life is miserable. Do not try to go somewhere else. Unless you change yourself, you will be stuck with your old circumstances and personality, from which there is no means to escape.

A person may lack motivation and interest in life. He might claim to want cultivation and enlightenment while being only half-hearted in his actions. He will make insincere promises to improve his career and relationships, and accordingly any actions he takes will be vague. These are indications that he lacks sufficient self-control, courage and responsibility and, due to the wrong cultivation methods, he has withdrawn the creativity of his mind.

Some psychologists, although unenlightened, can cure diseases—including cancer—through pure consultation. Regarding this, we Buddhists must reflect on ourselves: If our Buddha dharma is so beneficial, why could our practice not lead to the cure of diseases? Because all phenomena, including illness, is the creation of the Mind, why can we not achieve healing while those who are not enlightened can cure themselves? These psychological consultations may not use our self-control approach, but still they guide the patient to face his or her own thoughts, correct deviant character and lead his mind toward a more desirable direction. Regardless of whether or not the patient values enlightenment, the disease will be cured due to the fact that his or her mind has taken on a new direction and created a more optimistic, active attitude.

Many people carry on their cultivation in a state of limbo. They are neither truly committed to enlightenment nor willing to give up; they are neither confident that Nirvana will be attained nor content to go back to being mundane. These people have failed to make progress and have lost sight of the destination of their cultivation. Many initially practice spiritual cultivation with great aspiration for enlightenment, but eventually they are unsure as to what should be done with their lives. They may have dreamed of pursuing life's deeper meaning, but they no longer have sufficient courage to face it and accept the responsibility.

Live Your Life with Courage, Responsibility, Proactivity and Creativity

You should practice sitting meditation daily. Restrain any incorrect function of the mind while remaining aware that your mind is capable of creating a better outcome. It is, however, extremely difficult for the modern person to make a complete withdrawal from his or her attachments, so let us not discuss the distant, ultimate goal of liberation but focus instead on the present reality. It is not uncommon for a person to have practiced Buddhism for a long time but find that he is still burdened with issues of family, health and mental affliction. I often tell these people that both happiness and misery are their own creation, so no other individual can help. As the saying goes, "Heaven helps those who help themselves." If you do not create happiness, you will not have it. If you do not create freedom, you will not obtain it.

It is your own responsibility to create a better life.

If you cannot create the desired phenomena, it will be futile to wish for them. Therefore, we should have the idea of "creating" while using the right view of reality to withdraw the energy from our misguided creations. Know your bad habits and eliminate them through daily practice. Learn to use clear, positive thoughts instead of negative or deluded ones that will put your life in a state of limbo. Do everything completely, and restrain yourself fully. You must have such courage and inspiration to reach the "other shore." You want to be able to laugh when you want and make full use of your life's creative force.

Creativity lies in the Mind, so our goal is to use the Mind to generate the desired phenomena. Thus we practice creativity just as we train ourselves in self-control. The Mind is the source of everything, both positive and negative, and consequently the decision to have or not to have is made here. If you do not know how to create, practice it. Give rise to positive thoughts and compassion. When you are suffering, you should remind yourself that you are creating the suffering at that moment.

The Buddha, following his enlightenment, made an example of very proactive creation: He established the community of practitioners and spread the teachings to all beings. Even right up to his death, he remained actively engaged. Nowadays, young people want to retire early. They practice only during the day but not at night. The Buddha taught day and night, teaching all beings. Thus it is clear that most of us are not as engaged as the Buddha was. Many practitioners only focus on the aspect of self-control but ignore the significance of creativity. Now, however, we must pick up this power of creativity.

You only harvest what you sow, and your future depends on your effort. According to Buddhist teachings, one's health issues, family issues and cultivation issues are the karma that results from ignorance and ego attachment. Unaware that these issues are self-created, people stubbornly refuse to take responsibility. Instead, they try to find other answers and explanations despite being stuck in the problems they have created. Because your mind creates your problems, to resolve them you must refrain from seeking the truth outside the Mind, whereupon you must acknowledge and live with the acceptance of your karma. It is not real acceptance to accept something in resignation.

Stop seeking the truth outside yourself, from this moment on. Take responsibility for your own creation. Everything you see, hear or think of reveals the channel that is being opened in your mind. Because your mind is already creating in this way and manifesting everything accordingly, it is your only reality. Do not seek answers elsewhere. Diligently and actively make changes so that the mind can come alive, and thereby improve the inner condition of your mind. Then you can bring about better relationships and health in your outer reality.

What is the meaning of Buddhism if a practitioner cannot handle the most basic relationships and suffering in his reality? How can he have any chance of attaining enlightenment and liberation? Right now we are situated between two opposite shores of the flow of birth and death. We have departed from our shore but are unable to reach the opposite side. To resign yourself to a state of limbo—where the other shore seems so far, but returning to the past is not an option—will not solve any problems. Neither will there be any energy pushing you forward. Many practitioners have tried various sects of practices but ultimately say they just want to be reborn in the Pure Land. Why? They lack the self-confidence to complete the journey and have no direction for the future. It is easier, they think, to depend on other powers for rescue. They are unwilling to accept and take responsibility for their own karma.

I have asked many people why they believe in Christianity. They answer that Christianity is relatively simple: Once you have faith in God, all problems are solved. It is true that many people convert to Christianity for this reason. Buddhism, on the other hand, demands meditation and self-restraint. Its spiritual path seems full of hardship. In order to create a better future, a better karma, and a life of health and positivity, we must take on cultivation. This is so, because the ability is within us. We need to proactively make the effort to courageously face our personality flaws. We must practice self-control while using the creative force skillfully in order to make the changes necessary. By doing so, we can have a healthy, vibrant life.

> Realizing ability, purity and emptiness, the three disciples
> of Tang Sanzang kept themselves busy,
> Practicing self-discipline from greed,
> delusion and passion to find inner peace.
> Upon awakening they realized the journey was just a dream;
> India was still in the city of Chang'an.

9 APPLYING CULTIVATION PRINCIPLES TO DAILY LIFE

Autumn arrives and maple trees start to shed leaves;

Leaf after leaf, they drift in the sky like raindrops.

Leaning on the door I sighed with regret at the passing years;

The poet has ink but no roots.

Face Up to Your Reality

Cultivation is a process of inner transformation. First, you cultivate the ability of introspection, and then you find the way to dissolve the problem at its root. Ordinary people are not clear with their own thoughts. They constantly judge themselves as right or wrong and as good or bad. They are unaware that their feelings do not reflect reality but are instead moody reactions to external phenomena. Their thoughts develop along the paths set by their attachments, and this allows them little leeway in which to think differently. You must have room in which to re-evaluate your ideas, but most people have little or no doubt in regard to their own view of reality. They continue to use it as a guide.

People, in this world, are creators of positive karma and negative karma. For most of us, the creation of karma is the foundation of who we are. We are not the Buddha, the Bodhisattvas, saints or even truly dedicated spiritual people. Moreover, because our present state is a mixture of positive and negative, the mind still has many negative thoughts, not only in the sense of being dualistic but also in secular, moralistic terms.

Most people practice Buddhism based on habitual conditioning. In other words, such a person cultivates himself through the use of a very unstable, emotional state of mind. The human mind is not purely wholesome. A purely wholesome mind resonates with the karma of *devas,* or heavenly beings. Because we are not yet at the level of pure wholesomeness, there is considerable room for improvement. It is never the case that the moment a person converts to Buddhism, or any other religion, his contaminated personality will be elevated. There are different levels of beings among the *devas*, as there are with spirits and human beings. Any being whose karma confines it to the lavatory would be out of place when relocated to the prayer hall, because the lavatory is where his karma manifests. Just as in the spirit realm or the animal realm, human beings and *devas* are trapped in their own respective karmas.

Many people do not realize they have for so long been entrapped by their karmas. They may in fact feel very much at home within it. However, *devas* see us human beings the way we see maggots living in filth and stench. Our home is where our karma is. It is very difficult to escape from that home: our karma. You must first see your mind and karma so that you know where you stand. Otherwise, progress is not possible. If we have a twisted view of who we are in the present, we will not be able to elevate ourselves. The deepening of spiritual life cannot begin from a false point of departure. It is not easy to face our true self. So, if we manage to do that, we are about to make genuine progress.

The occurrence of positive and negative thoughts leads to a

mixture of wholesome and unwholesome actions. That is the basis of being human, but if we do not uplift the basis in this lifetime we will be reincarnated into similar conditions. There are many practitioners now, but few can face themselves honestly. We should first recognize the fact that we will never get close to transcending duality if we are unable to attain a wholesome state of being.

Spiritual practice is about counteracting and dissolving our afflictions and delusions. Someone once told me, "Because the Mind encompasses all realms and all phenomena are merely due to consciousness, we need to establish a positive frame of mind in order to dispel negative thoughts that cause misfortune and negative karma." However, in reality much of the so-called positive thinking is based on greed, anger and attachment. The "I" with which anyone is identified is simply that person's body and thoughts. From this little "I," filled with attachment and hampered by narrow-mindedness, we try unsuccessfully to contrive positive thinking.

Despite positive motivations, a blurred mind that is based on that little "I" and burdened by negativity cannot function in a clear, positive way. Thus the so-called positive thinking is really a disguise of the shadows within our personality. Every effort based on that kind of thinking will be in vain, because such positive thinking is not grounded in the truth of who we are.

Many people fail to appreciate the infinite potential of the Mind. Even those who do appreciate it will rarely choose to be happy when negative emotions arise. The capacity of one's mind is limited by attachment because there is a false notion of "I." It is created from the karmic basis of being human, consisting of attachment, right and wrong thinking and self-versus-other dualities. To achieve enlightenment from such a basis is as difficult as a worm's attempt to evolve into a mammal or an animal into a human. Such an analogy may not be pleasant to consider, but it illustrates the old saying, "It is easy to move the mountains and rivers but hard to change one's nature."

Look at yourself honestly and ask, given your current state of mind, about your commitment to cultivation, your character and merit. What would your next incarnation be like? Could you become a *deva*? Recognize the truth of where you are, but do not underestimate the effort involved in spiritual cultivation. No significant change in life will come from daydreaming.

People tend to study Buddhism as if it were a subject such as engineering or literature, or as if it were a kind of character training such as discussed in Confucianism. In reality, such people are far removed from genuine spiritual cultivation. One can talk about the theories of engineering or the computations involved in mathematics. If you study Buddhism this way, you will certainly know about the theory of karma, bodhi, enlightenment, the three pitiful transmigrations, the need to cultivate good and restrain evil, impermanence, dependent origination, etc. However, in that case you are treating Buddhism as a kind of technical knowledge.

Is your knowledge of engineering or literature in any way helpful to your state of mind? Can such knowledge dissolve your attachments and vexations? If not, how can you expect any knowledge of Buddhism thus acquired to eradicate your attachments? The memorization of Buddhist jargon does not equate to true spiritual progress. The real problem is that despite such supposed knowledge one cannot attain even the lowest state of the heavenly realm. Some people claim they will not come back here in their next life as a human being. However, if they do not come back here, then where will they go? It is very likely that they will be reincarnated with the same old karma.

It Is Painful to Face Oneself

Someone once said that soon after their arrival in the U.S., many masters of the Mahayana tradition became immersed in the Chinese-speaking communities and consequently their teachings were not widely propagated. However, both Theravada and Tibetan Buddhists have published many written materials in English because their adherents, having arrived in the U.S., did not receive the kind of support from an immigrant population and therefore immediately began to teach the English-speaking community. This is not true. The Sixth Patriarch Hui Neng was illiterate, so why did he have so many disciples? The contemporary, Master Guang Qin, delivered few lectures and authored few teaching materials. Why did so many practitioners follow him? In America, many Tibetan Buddhist masters do not speak a single word of English: Why are many of their students Americans? The key is the degree of realization, not the words.

Buddhist dharma can be promoted through words, but promotion alone will not attract audiences. Successful, beneficial propagation is not exclusively dependent on the amount of teaching materials or the proficiency of English. The real issue is whether we have sufficient realization and spiritual strength to benefit people. Mahayana teaching places a greater emphasis on charity but less on freeing all beings from transmigrations. This balance is partly due to the historical conflicts among Confucianism, Buddhism and Daoism in China, which hindered the development of the focus toward liberation. However, the real reason lies in whether we have gone far enough in practicing what we preach or, in other words, dissolving our mental hindrances. There are many preaching and ritual practices, but clearly the degree of inner transformation and purification is insufficient. We must reflect on this and correct it.

If a phenomenon generated by the Mind is limited by the notion of a little "I," it will neither have a broad impact nor make a significant leap forward. The pure, clear Mind enables Buddha to manifest various realms simultaneously. However, the ordinary mind is impeded by the petty ego. The ordinary-minded person is confined to his family and career; he is bound by karma to live within his attachments. Unaware of the impediments of his karma, he wastes time and effort repeating the same mistakes over and over throughout his life. Thus we have the saying, "A horse grows his teeth to no avail." A horse grows a new tooth each year, but each year he keeps doing the same backbreaking labor. Similarly, if a person repeats the same unhealthy pattern of his attachment year after year, in the long term what will he create that is positive and worthwhile? Most people's minds repeatedly create phenomena and their related problems without ever being able to escape them.

It is somewhat cruel having to face oneself, know oneself and then negate oneself. Xiang Yan was speechless when Master Gui Shan asked him, "What was it like before you were born to your parents?" Despite all his learning, he could not muster a response. He could not conceive, nor could he let go of, even a single question. He burned his scriptures and departed from the temple in tears, because he had finally come face to face with himself and realized that everything he had learned was useless. We, who have nowhere near the practice, learning and intelligence of Xiang Yan, are no match for even his unenlightened self. We are not ready to let go.

Why must the Zen masters so completely shatter attachment? It is because this is the only way to be reborn. Thus it is said, "Beat your delusory thinking to death in order to give life to your dharma body."

How cruel is it to face oneself? I tell you now: The mind with which you understand my teaching is deluded. What you know is rubbish; it is useless in regard to your problems. Learning with an impure mind only results in impurity, so that education is useless. This is your current condition. This is a fairly cruel method of delivery, but it is the truth. Do you know who you are? Certainly, you do not. Have you been enlightened? You have not. Is your mind full of vexations? Yes, it is. Many people are not ready to face themselves, so how can they hope to progress?

Someone once asked me, "Is disease karma?" Yes, of course it is. "Is karma created by the Mind?" Yes, of course. We practice Buddhism for quite some time, but still we cannot cure our own diseases. Why is that so? It is because the learning we treasure and believe is illusory, like "calling a yellow leaf gold so as to distract a child from crying." The opinions and knowledge in a person's mind amount to nothing but a pile of yellow leaves. They trick him into feeling wealthy, like a king.

We deceive ourselves with our opinions and perceptions regarding our environment. For example, we think this food tastes good and that food tastes bad, or this person is good but that person is bad. These opinions and perceptions are based on ego and karma. Here is a way to inspect yourself: When you are upset, see if you can dissolve that feeling all by yourself—truly by yourself—without resorting to music, movies, books or conversation. If your mind can dissolve negativities by itself, it means you are less dependent on your environment. If you cannot uplift yourself without external stimuli —by talking with or thinking about others, listening to something, feeling something or holding onto certain external people, situations or objects—you still have a long way to go.

Progress Comes from Facing Up to Yourself

Real progress cannot be attained without facing yourself. Why does it take such a long time to obtain the benefit of spiritual practice? It takes a long time when there is no real learning, such as when you treat practice like an academic subject and learn it only superficially. The new content in my teaching makes the learning process seem more pleasant, but my repeated teachings about the Mind bring complaints. You do not realize that every lecture about the Mind is new, since you perceive it as something old. Because the attachment in your mind remains unchanged, you cannot hear anything new. To deviate from the Mind is to seek truth outside oneself, but people enjoy learning and listening to various things. They accumulate all sorts of knowledge about all kinds of things, and they always want something different. When listening, looking and thinking, however, we must use the Mind. Nothing is outside the Mind.

It is not possible to go anywhere if the mind cannot regain its independence from phenomena or is plagued by attachment. It is possible to train a parrot to recite, "I pay homage to Amida Buddha," but that does not make the parrot a spiritual practitioner. Many a person, having gained some knowledge, might talk day in and day out about the Five Commandments and the Ten Good Actions. However, if such a person cannot practice what he preaches, how is he different from a parrot that mimics Buddhist chanting? Do not talk continually about principles that you do not diligently practice. Without real efforts, how can one be reincarnated as a beautiful, pure *deva,* not to mention achieving enlightenment? Because we are still human beings, it would be more practical to think about how to become a better person first.

The Tang poet Bai Juyi once paid a visit to Master Niao Ke and asked to learn the gist of the Buddha dharma. Master Niao Ke simply said, "Do no evil deeds; do all good deeds." Bai Juyi was a devout Buddhist who had studied long and hard with many masters, but he could only laugh: "How could this be the gist of Buddha dharma? Even a three-year-old knows that principle!" As with Bai Juyi, many followers believe they already know all about refraining from evil and generating compassion, etc., so they ask their masters to teach them enlightenment. I know you want to become enlightened, but first we must accomplish the fundamentals!

Master Niao Ke then said, "What a three-year-old knows, an eighty-year-old cannot do." What does that mean? From birth to death, all our learning cannot even deliver us to the next level. We remain within the human realm. We are still far from Buddhahood, much like the way that the maggots in feces are still far from the reality of the human realm and its many challenges. Therefore, until you devote true effort toward cultivation you should not even think about reaching enlightenment.

Buddha's disciples were able to achieve enlightenment in their respective lifetimes because they spent all their time facing up to themselves and dealing with their inadequacies. Have we spent every moment elevating ourselves and dissolving our vexations? Real effort is not possible unless we stop giving our energy to conflicts and judgments. Even the exceptionally diligent and focused Master Xiang Yan was reduced to tears at the moment he was compelled to face himself. People today think highly of themselves, even though their bodies, minds and realities are anything but pure.

The one who is ignorant is unaware of his ignorance. Those who have suffered are not aware that they have done so. We are trapped in our own issues but cannot see them. This is the karma of humanity. The unenlightened person, not knowing where he is and where he is going, nevertheless says meaningless things such as, "I will go to the Western Paradise; I will not be back here in my next life." One day, when you truly face yourself, tears will be the least of the struggle. If you are not yet in tears, you are probably not yet prepared for real cultivation. Unless you are prepared to face yourself, you cannot transform your karma. Face the truth within you, and then you will see true progress.

All the teachings are for the purpose of curing the illnesses of the mind. The lack of progress does not belong to Buddha. It rests on your readiness to face yourself. It is cruel but absolutely essential to face yourself. Do not indulge yourself by staying in your limited world. People, like pigs, cows, cats and dogs, find comfort in their lairs. But to stay in your lair is to be held captive by your old karma.

Take one step at a time as you face your true self. Do not aim higher than you can reach, nor disparage the little acts of good. Having cultivated yourself for so long, why do your issues remain unresolved? Why have you failed to dissolve your disease and the trouble created by your own mind and karma? The answer is that you do not know your mind. You have never made an effort to face your sick, troubled self.

Buddhist scriptures teach us the Five Commandments, the Six Bodhisattva Practices and the Ten Good Actions because we do not have them. They are not just academic knowledge but are instead principles that must be internalized through hard work. Buddha dharma has pointed out for us what we must improve upon and learn. In this context, learning refers to spiritual elevation. It does not mean using our attachment to accumulate even more attachments.

Identify your problems first. Next, face yourself and, with the guidance of Buddha dharma, constantly cultivate yourself. Remember this simple rule: If you cannot dissolve worry and frustration without resorting to external conditions and stimulations, such inability indicates that your mind lacks self-sufficiency and is too dependent on external phenomena. When your mind is in this state, it is unable to transform its vexations. Your vexations will only increase, making significant progress extremely difficult to achieve.

How could a human blade cut the cake of emptiness?

The heaven above is painted with our ancestral saints.

Buddha's mercy defeated Sakyamuni;

Do not recognize the Buddha nature in all.

10 THE SPONGE-MIND EFFECT

My mother, so intelligent, was a Cambridge student;

Your father, how handsome, graduated from Oxford.

Due to a longstanding grudge, our families ended interactions;

Little did we know that we hurt no one else but ourselves.

Habitual Patterns Do Not Change Easily

Many people have commented that my teaching is profound and unique. If that is the case, why do some of my students behave as if they are not really benefiting from my teaching or practicing my teachings in their daily lives? Whether in religious practice or psychological consultation, many people seem to have the same issue: They understand what they hear but they can neither explain it nor apply it in life. Some people are very motivated after they attend one of my lectures, and they practice diligently, but still they are easily defeated by challenges. This situation is very similar to that of a person who learns kung fu deep in the mountains and one day sets out to save the world, only to be defeated by the first challenge he encounters. The point is that knowing is not the same as doing. Even when you believe you can, your belief may still be superficial or pretentious.

New learning often provokes new ideas, but how deep are these new ideas and how frequently do they arise? Temporary thoughts, as opposed to firm convictions, do not inspire real change. You can be touched and inspired by a lecture but easily forget all about it once you return home. Ideas are like tools. The old, frequently used ones are our habits, while the newly obtained ones are not yet firmly established in the mind. We fail to make much use of these new tools. Even though new lessons may be inspiring to us, the new ideas are still registered in the surface level of the mind. Your deeply ingrained ideas are like the things around you. They are easily accessible. The ideas that are not so deeply ingrained in you are not as accessible, like tools that are kept in storage. The old ideas we use each day, despite being very accessible, are difficult to change.

A new idea is like a stranger: Even though you had a good chat with him and developed a positive feeling, it will still take a while until you feel comfortable enough to invite him home. Thus the key to learning is to transform a new idea into an applicable conviction. Aimless learning is merely an accumulation of knowledge that is disconnected from the thought habits that control your real life. People normally take for granted what habitually and naturally goes on in their lives, so they do not stop to understand or analyze them. Habit is the number-two master of your life, and it is difficult to overcome. Stubborn, deeply rooted habits are major obstacles to the internalization of new ideas.

Habitual thinking forms stereotypes, and the older you get the more fixed your stereotypes become. Just as you are most unlikely to rearrange your home furniture from day to day, the mind's reluctance to change is the same. However, a lack of change in the external environment means there is little movement of the inner environment and therefore little space for new ideas. Even when your mind does absorb new ideas, it does so through the old channels. Therefore, only the aspects that suit the old channels in the mind can be received. You prefer to eat, hear and do certain things; you prefer to associate with certain kinds of people. Your inner environment is set in its ways and much more difficult to change than you realize. All the phenomena generated through such a mind are also well set and lacking in freshness.

The functions of the Mind include a person's thoughts, behaviors and various perceptions. The perspective of your mind determines the location from which things are observed, which in turn determines what you see, hear and experience. When you read my teaching, what and how much you hear is specifically determined by the unique perspective within your mind. You cannot see any more or less than what your mind is capable of perceiving through its filters. Accordingly, the important thing is not what you hear or see but to find out exactly where you are in the first place. Only if you know where you are can real change be accomplished.

Our perception is part of the environment, just as the observer is. The location of the observer has already determined what can be observed. Perception is energy, and body is energy. The inner environment of the mind determines the energy that will resonate with us. Energy is indivisible, and consequently we cannot say that the people or environment we perceive have nothing to do with us. Years ago, the place where I used to lecture was just an open space with neither buildings nor roads. Then people gradually moved in, built houses and roads. These roads now confine where people can travel. The preset ideas in your mind are like those roads: They limit the freedom of your mind. When change surpasses the limitation, we become flexible. When the limitation overpowers change, we become rigid.

Squeeze the Presumption from the Sponge

Everyone has thoughts. As for the validity of anyone's thoughts, different people have different opinions. Buddhists, Christians and Muslims all claim their own religion to be the truth. In family life, you, your spouse and even your children may all claim to have more valid viewpoints. In a relativistic world, this self-righteousness stands as a trait common to all.

Outside your mind there are roads, but inside your mind there are also tracks. Can you produce a thought that is not within the confines of those mind tracks? The answer is probably no, unless you have been subjected to some intense shock or revelation, but such occasions are rare in life. The mind tracks set up your reaction to the world, which has no issue otherwise. The real issue always rests with the tracks in your mind. They determine what kinds of people, situations and difficulties will appear in your life. The relationship between your mind and your reality is such that everything corresponds to you.

It is as difficult to learn new ideas through the filter of a rigid mind frame as it is to absorb nutrition with a body that suffers from various blockages. We must first cleanse the body's blockage and improve its condition before it can be nourished. Similarly, you must know yourself first. See how you limit your own mind and how it can be released.

People live in their habits, which are defined by their thought patterns. We rarely, if ever, reflect on them. Here is a story about a husband and a wife: At each meal, no matter how hot the soup was, the husband would finish it with one long gulp. His wife asked him how he managed to do that. The husband simply replied, "It's a secret." One day, the wife prepared a feast and warmly pressed him more about this habit. He said, "Because my grandfather did it, my father did it, so I do it too. There must be a good reason for it, so I also do it."

This is the man's so-called secret. There are many secrets that people hold close to heart to make them feel more capable. Once you learn and internalize an idea, you are obliged to keep it and use it unless you have the ability to substitute it with another one. If you cannot replace the thoughts in your mind with new ones, it is impossible to make progress in spiritual cultivation because you cannot digest what has been learned. There must first be the dissolution of ideas before something new can emerge. By dissolving your presumptions, your mind acquires the capacity to receive and learn.

Many people's convictions are fixed and difficult to change. Furthermore, close inspection reveals that they usually turn out to be the echoing other people's ideas. Many people believe Buddhism talks about suffering and that it is overly pessimistic. However, does the optimism of these people make a real impact? Self-hypnosis does not lead to change. In order to make progress, we must have self-understanding, self-responsibility and self-cultivation. If we do not clearly recognize ourselves, how can the deluded self attain new understanding? Many practitioners never truly change their behavior and thought patterns. How can we help others if we do not first transform our beliefs and actions and thereby elevate ourselves?

Sometimes, when you are in a tough situation, your family and friends will come forward with advice and ideas on what they think should be done. You might find it curious: If these advisers are not faring any better in their own lives, how effective can their advice be? If you follow their ideas, the best outcome is to end up like them; if you follow your own idea, then you are already where you are. If you cannot transform your own issues, you should not offer suggestions to others. You really do not know what you are talking about.

Cultivation has definite steps. First, you must loosen the rigidity inside the mind so that it can absorb new information. The Mind is like a sponge: When it is soaked with water, even if you immerse it in the ocean of knowledge it will not absorb much more, except on the very surface layer. If your thinking is not opened up, new ideas cannot be received and utilized. Your current ideas not only take up space in your mind but also reinforce and consolidate your current mind frame. Thoughts get stronger as you continue to use them until they cannot be controlled. Life's problems do not come about or disappear based on your wishes. Instead, they are determined by the thoughts that occupy your mind. They are always with you, and they form the foundation of your life. The result of these habitual tendencies in the mind is the "sponge-mind effect."

The question of whether or not a new idea can materialize depends on whether it actually enters the mind. While some ideas may seem well understood, true understanding comes only when it becomes a reality in action. Otherwise, it is nothing but belief. You can keep telling your son not to come home late because it is dangerous, but he may say, "Yes, I know," and still come home at midnight.

Spiritual growth is the process of opening up the self instead of externally accumulating knowledge. This is why some people, having learned the same principle, become more and more open-minded while others become increasingly rigid. Buddha dharma is the teaching of wisdom, but truth is still the truth regardless of who says it. The question is how we can apply it. Therefore, it is more important to know yourself than it is to obtain new knowledge. Dissolve the inner structure of attachment so that your mind will have more room for growth.

If you believe in the benefit of spiritual cultivation, what benefit have you received from it? Perhaps you have received some, or maybe you have received nothing at all. The external reality is the extension of your inner thoughts. Therefore, do not make superficial judgments about whether you want something or not, or whether something is good or not. These surface appearances are far from your actual inner mindscape. They are not the thought habits and behaviors you frequently use. What you use each day is what you use without consideration. In other words, these are what Buddhism calls "habitual tendencies." When you think someone or something is annoying, the truth is that "you" make him annoying. "You" make the situation an issue and suffer because of it. The "annoying" person may have no clue of what is going on in your mind. He might simply behave in his usual way, while you suffer the misery of the issue you have created.

Affirm Yourself, Negate Yourself

A man went to the market on his brand-new bicycle. The market was right next to the village temple, so he parked his bike under the banyan tree in front of the temple. After grocery shopping, he walked back to his home, which was not very far, and forgot to ride the bike home. The next morning, as he got ready to start out, he realized that he had left his bicycle by the banyan tree. He rushed back to the temple and, to his great delight, his bike was right where he had left it. Crediting this good fortune to the village deity, he walked into the temple to show his gratitude and pay respect. Then, when he stepped out, his bike was gone.

Heaven helps those who help themselves. Spiritual growth comes to the one whose mind is flexible and free of fixed thinking. No matter what happens, your mind frame always creates certain interpretations and desires in response to the situation. If that desire is not yet satisfied, the mind frame that created the desire cannot be released and you will be stuck in the middle. You feel as if the external environment is oppressing you. Your suffering comes from the fact that you cannot use your mind flexibly or demonstrate the understanding that all external phenomena are triggered by your inner mindset.

The first step in handling any problem is to identify the underlying mindset. Your present mindset and actions already determine the situation thus created, since this is your reality. Buddha, Bodhisattva, the scriptures and theories are only raw materials with which you can work. You become the material you will use for learning. Consider politics, for example. Initially, you are not interested in politics, so your mind is as indifferent as a dry sponge. However, the instant you generate an initial favorable opinion about a political party, the thought immediately develops a track in your mindscape. Based on that track in the mind, you will repeatedly form the same favorable opinion regarding that party. This pattern perpetuates itself until you become so hypnotized in the correctness of your opinion that you become a supporter of that party.

The generation of the first thought is like the moment one's eyes are first opened: What you see will trigger a reaction and set the tone for what comes next. Learning is actually a process of self-hypnosis. When you have a certain thought, it determines your position as the observer and how the observed phenomena will be manifested. Man is intrigued by the appearances he attracts with his current mindset, and he continues to grasp and encourage similar thoughts and appearances. A continuous stream of similar thoughts and similar paths in the mind creates our thinking and beliefs. Naturally, a sponge soaked in water smells like water; only after the water is squeezed out can the sponge absorb another liquid and another scent.

This is the heart of the matter: Man does not believe in religion or theories but instead believes in himself. Because it is all about your belief and opinion, what does it have to do with God and Buddha? The external is utterly connected to the internal. Zen teaches that outside the Mind there is no world; that the world is as the Mind is. Therefore, in order to change the world you must first change your mind.

People often say, "I am who I am," but most people do not know their true selves. It is more accurate to say, "I am who I have made myself to be." Ultimately, you are not just this way. You can be much greater and bigger. Thus it is a very limiting belief to think, "This is the way I am." Each thought you have is a tool with which to create wholesomeness in life, but it is not the only way you must be. When there is anger and you believe you are angry but do not realize the source of life, you have allowed that belief to limit you.

Mind is formless, and therefore the mastery of the mind means the mastery of its function. If you can laugh, cry, remain calm and free of vexation whenever you want, it shows mastery over the Mind's function. Mastery only comes from the self, and the self is the master of the Land of Bliss. Buddhist teaching is predicated on making efforts in creation; it is not predicated on making efforts so that others will rescue you.

Humans have human issues, of course. A student once asked me how to get rid of human issues, to which I gave an easy answer: Just stop being human. This is the truth, not a joke. When your thoughts create corresponding problems, the proper way to deal with those problems is to tackle the thoughts that created them. I often use a simple analogy: A lumberjack uses his ax to chop down a tree. However, if he uses the ax to cook it will certainly get in the way. So, the right thing to do is to put down the ax. Our emotions and beliefs are tools, but often we cannot put them away despite their inappropriateness for the task. Even the best tool can become a burden if it cannot solve one's problems.

You have the ability to live a better life, but it depends on your wise use of life's various tools. The key to relaxing the rigid mentality is to first realize that thoughts, emotions and knowledge are all life's tools. We as human beings are their masters, not their slaves. The so-called "I" is simply a collection of habitual thoughts. If such thoughts cannot bring you a better life, it is time to set them aside. It is you who gives your sponge-mind a certain smell and then insists on the rightness of that smell. However, this smell is not the nature of who you are. You need to squeeze the sponge dry so that it can absorb something new. You should let anything go, once it is done.

I have, during my time in the U.S., witnessed many situations in which a person has lost his common sense after converting to a religion. Now, I am not advocating the use of common sense to judge all ideas. In fact, if one uses only common sense to judge everything, there is no chance that change will occur. However, it is a pity that when people accept new ideas they can lose their common sense.

Some of you may ask whether it is better to delve deep into a particular spiritual teaching or to sample and learn extensively. When you look at the world from behind a door, no matter how many ways you try to look, your view will be no wider than the gap in that door. Therefore, it is futile to learn extensively without dissolving the egoistic structure of your limiting belief. However, when your attachment is deeply rooted, delving into one spiritual teaching will only reinforce the attachment. To solve the dilemma, you must first compose the mind and calm its habitual tendencies. With that done, better results can be achieved as you strive for depth or breadth.

You must affirm yourself as well as negate yourself in order to elevate yourself to a certain degree. What is there to affirm? You must affirm the innate Mind, whose infinite creativity and energy can complete and manifest the reality that corresponds to your thoughts. If you do not trust the fact that you possess the ability to change, you will not try your best. In fact, you might as well not try. However, if you do believe you have the ability to change, you must make effort. If you do not affirm your ability to change, you will expect others to rescue you and free you from your pains and struggles. This is like waiting for fruit to fall from the sky instead of planting the seeds and cultivating yourself. What is there to negate? You must realize that you are what you are because you have used your mind's ability in the wrong way. This pattern of misuse should be negated.

The Mind is like a mother who has unconditionally loved and supported you from the past to the present and will continue to do so in the future. Your current difficulties are the result of your misuse of the resources and support your mother has given you. Therefore, you must correct yourself. You must also negate yourself—meaning the misused functions—but not negate the ability to function.

Today, it is popular to "educate children with love." However, one must be careful not to spoil the child and expand his ego out of proportion to the point that he cannot accept adversity, stress and the need to correct his own errors. Children sometimes need encouragement, and sometimes they need guidance and correction. It is misleading and harmful to shower a child with praise when he is headed down the wrong road. A child's mind frame is immature, and consequently we must nurture it and guide it. Similarly, in the grand universe we humans are children. We need to learn to find our way without clinging too tightly to what we believe.

The wise know the truth and live according to its principles. The Mind is for you to use, but it allows you to misuse it as well. The Mind can produce flexibility but also rigidity. If the Mind can generate any thought, why does it not generate the thought you want? It is because your mind has been conditioned. It has become rigid. Can you change the mind? Yes, of course you can. You have the ability to make yourself into who you are today, so you certainly have the ability to recreate yourself in other ways.

A Zen master was once invited to bless a grandfather's birthday celebration. The master wrote, "Grandfather dies, father dies; son dies, grandson dies." The grandfather was very upset by this ominous verse, but the master gave an explanation: "What is written here is indeed a blessing. Is it not a natural and perfect outcome for the grandfather to die first and then the father, then the son and lastly the grandson? If this order were reversed, would not that bring a great deal of pain?" To elevate life, one must follow the principle of life to create a good life.

Give encouragement to yourself when you do things right, because doing things right shows that your mind, like a mother, is very wise. When you do things wrong, it means the mind is not so wise and has indulged in erroneous ways. Whether you are optimistic or pessimistic, your life will not change until you truly understand how life functions and manifests. With that understanding, you will have the chance to change your life and shape your future.

I give you an apple, but you want a pear;
Moving the flowers and grafting the trees
produces strange flavors.
It would be best to start over in the field;
This way one has control over one's own fate.

11 DISSOLVE STRESS IN LIFE WITH ZEN

Thousand-foot waterfall flows into a deep pond;

High waves hit off the bank and splash onto devas.

Behind the water a bird flies back to its nest in a tree;

Unencumbered by the four seasons the flower of

the self is always in spring.

Ordinary Happiness Is Based on a Very Narrow Set of Conditions

People face stress from the day they are born into this world. Babies feel stress if they do not see their mothers or get milk when they are hungry. Elementary students face the stress of school work and extracurricular activities as well as the reactions from parents and teachers. Secondary students are stressed about passing college entrance examinations and the pursuit of additional studies. College students are stressed about finding jobs, and professionals are stressed about office relationships, salaries, traffic jams, working overtime, bringing work home and causing agitation within their families.

Marriage is considered a must in countries such as China. People must bear the pressure to get married because it is not socially acceptable to remain single. However, being married also comes with many chores and considerable stress. There is the stress of becoming parents and even grandparents. In the end, when it is time to depart this world, people face the fear and stress of the uncertainty of death.

Life is filled with pressure. The completion of one stage in life merely ushers in another stage with its respective goals and stresses.

An ancient poem goes like this: "All day I felt sleepy and dreamy; but suddenly it dawned on me that spring was coming to an end, so I forced myself to take a hike. By sheer chance I passed a temple and overheard some Zen talk; it gave me yet another half-day's leisure in this floating life." Everyone wants to be free of stress. In the U.S., some people like to take a break from work and drive a long way with the whole family just to find a beach and sunbathe. The mindset of vacationing is, more or less, to simply create an opportunity to get away from the usual environment and daily pressure.

I often tell my students that I am fortunate to live in the simple, stable environment of a temple. After all, in this world it is not easy to find a refuge for the mind and body. While it is relatively easy to obtain enjoyment from food and clothing in the mundane world, it is very difficult to attain the pure enjoyment that a stable, worry-free mind can offer. However, from a different perspective we can see that not everyone can have a materially abundant lifestyle, although each of us has the potential to obtain pure enjoyment as long as the mind is peaceful and tranquil. Some people pursue money, but inadvertently they also pursue the worries that come with wealth. People tend to see only the desirable aspect of a reality but ignore or remain unaware of the undesirable aspect of what they actively seek. They do not perceive the fact that, despite wealth and fame, there will be frustration and trouble. Therefore, happiness in life should be understood from many different perspectives.

We human beings have vast networks of relationships. Each

thought, every cell and every person around us is connected to our life. Even material things have a relationship with us: The broken faucet, a stained rug or a torn couch can cause one to feel vexation. Consequently, a relationship is not just between people. The situation and physical environment around us are included, too. Defects in any single relationship can bring us affliction. A life that is perfect and stable calls for perfection and stability in every relationship. The happiness most people pursue, however, is based on a narrow set of conditions in which many aspects of practical reality are ignored. The scope of our mind activity is generally habitual, and accordingly we tend to consider only the relationships with either our favored or undesirable people and situations. Our thoughts represent our habitual relationships. The truth is that there is a connection between you and each phenomenon in your life, including thoughts you have not previously had. The true nature of life's phenomena is based on relationships.

We define ourselves by our rigid thoughts, and we come to know ourselves by these rigid thoughts. As ego becomes inflated and stronger, it divides the wholeness of life and all its relationships into an inner "I-consciousness" and an external body. It locks in the idea that this small fragment of the entire reality—the I-consciousness—is our self. When we lock the self into this definition, we cut ourselves off from the true existence of all life's relationships. In reality, what we consider unrelated to our limited sense of self is still a relationship that can bring us happiness or suffering.

The Mind is the source of life. It has the ability to manifest the true relationship of our life as a whole. Thus the fragmentation of this wholeness will lead to illusory gaps and distinctions in life, which turn into stress and suffering. To understand the stress of life, one must learn to see life as a whole instead of seeing it as a scattering of isolated pieces. When a relationship is manifested by the Mind, do not bother to figure out whether and how it is related to you, because it already is. Any discrimination you make is simply the deluded function of your ego and its attachment. Reality does not require your definition, because it exists as it has manifested and is already complete in this moment. The Mind can directly know the reality as it manifests, so you do not need to "know" reality again through your thinking and judgment. Our mind capacity is vast, so do not box yourself into your own thoughts. Liberation is not the pursuit of something but is instead the release of your ego's attachment.

Stress Happens When Our Attachments Are in Conflict With Life as a Whole

A river that is blocked will shift course and continue its flow toward a different outlet. Similarly, stress is the force that propels life to unfold. When a person's ego tries to impose its small notion of self onto the network of relationships in life's reality, a great deal of stress is created. As our personality tries to navigate in and out of this wholeness, it encounters various obstructions that turn into stress. Stress also drives your life in a certain direction. When you are not under pressure, a happy thought can come with a smile. In that case, you can directly feel the function of your mind because your ego is not strong. When your supervisor scolds you or when you disagree with others, you may feel obliged to smile. Such a smile, however, is not the direct, natural outcome of your mind state. Instead, it is the work of pressure. Such a smile is actually harmful to your health. It is not true that having a smiling face is always indicative of goodness.

Annoyance and the faults we see in others actually reflect the annoyance and faults in ourselves, but people do not see this. I once told a practitioner that, if one sees the faults of others, it means one has faults. She was stressed and felt that the fault clearly lay in others, not in herself. Therefore, you should first try to set aside your thinking and consider the reason you cannot see the rightness in other people's actions. This question is worthy of further consideration. If your spouse misbehaves, there is actually a part of the misbehavior that belongs to you. If your spouse has a problem, you cannot say it is unrelated to you because it already is related to you. If you do not see the positive side, it is because you cannot see ways to improve your relationship with your spouse. The failure to recognize how broadly everything is interconnected will confine you and make it hard to elevate yourself.

It was once said, "If men possess sincerity, the Buddha becomes responsive." In other words, the lack of response indicates a lack of sincerity. People may think they are sincere at heart but do not understand why the desired reality is not manifested. It is possible that their sincerity is forced by certain concerns or worries that are very negative. This underlying negativity is the real motivator in their life. Your true motivation is the force behind life's unfolding process. Both Buddha dharma and your masters tell you that external flaws reflect inner flaws, but deep within your heart do you really believe it? Your ego might disagree. Having a thought that is a direct, uncontrived laugh will bring all kinds of benefits to your body. Many people, however, are not so straightforward. In their hearts, there are deep attachments and motives that have not been released, despite the fact they were told to change so that they could learn within this tension. The result of their learning is the result of this tension. It is a mixed outcome driven by the apparent goal of the teaching and a conflicting, unconscious desire underneath. Nevertheless, the direct power of the mind should be the basis of one's life.

The capacity of the Mind is limitless. However, when limitless appearances are projected by the Mind, people usually identify a minor portion of it as the self and treat the rest as external. Thus they are unable to experience integration. In every moment, life is a whole. Our relationship with time, space and situations is the one true Collective. If you do not see how vast and comprehensive life is, you cannot perfect the wholeness of life.

Ancient Buddhists first acknowledged life as a whole and then worked on dissolving the ego that prevented them from embracing the whole of life. The saints achieved their goal through self-control as they withdrew their erroneous I-consciousness. "Everyone can be a saint; everyone has Buddha nature." These are concepts of self-control. Once we attain this realization, we will not direct our effort toward the expansion of ego. Spiritual cultivation therefore begins with self-control, which on one hand seems to curb creativity. On the other hand, what good can creativity manifest without true wisdom? Wisdom always precedes the creation of what is appropriate and beneficial. Therefore, the ancient Buddhists first practiced self-control and cultivated wisdom before they engaged in helping others. This sequence demonstrates that the correct process starts by dispelling the conflict within ourselves as we restrain the expansion of ego. However, many modern methods fail to release us from stress: Vacationing, shopping, eating out or venting emotions only diverts the mind from one function to another. The stress will return as soon as this person returns to his or her normal state. These methods fail because they do not stop the ego from dissecting the wholeness of life.

Ego attachment clings to various things as it moves from one object to another and different emotions are evoked. No matter how you change the object to which you cling, as long as the force of ego attachment is present, you cannot experience the Collective. Stress will be released only when you release the ego attachment and see life as a whole.

There is originally no stress in a person's mind until his habits and beliefs compel him to think and react in a certain way without the choice to do otherwise. In the mind there are many "musts," because this world of appearances is the product of the mind. Inevitably there are many musts in this world as well. These musts bring stress and suffering. If we do not recognize the stress caused by our self-attachment and the resulting phenomena that prevent our life from unfolding—the stress by which we are unable to dissolve the inevitable attachment and its personality traits—we cannot dissolve life's musts.

The Empty Mind Holds No Stress

Once there was a person who had a pile of dung on the tip of his nose. Searching everywhere, he smelled the stench but could not find the source. Finally he came upon a mirror and saw the dung on his nose. After wiping away the source of the odor, the stench was gone for good. If we do not find the source, the problem cannot be solved by looking here and there. Applying some perfume does not improve the odor, either. In this story, the tip of the nose represents the source of life. Life that unfolds from certain core beliefs will intimately reflect those beliefs in its phenomena.

Tang Zen Master Gu Ling, having achieved enlightenment, went back to pay gratitude to his old master who, at the time, was not yet enlightened. The master asked him what he had learned after all the years. Gu Ling said, "Nothing." Hearing this, his master promptly assigned some chores to him. One day, while giving the master a bath, Gu Ling said, "What a great prayer hall! It's a pity that the Buddha is not sacred." Real Buddhists try to recognize and unfold Buddha in their lives; in other words, they seek the real Buddha in the Mind, not an external Buddha. The master was puzzled by Gu Ling's words, so he turned to him and stared. Gu Ling continued, "Although not sacred, the Buddha still shines light." Gu Ling's verse implied that the Mind is what "everyone uses daily without awareness." Without knowing the Mind you can still talk, walk, laugh and cry. These are all functions of the Mind.

Another day, Gu Ling found his master reading scriptures. At the time, a bee was flying back and forth in the room as it searched for a way out. The door was wide open, but the windows were sealed with paper; the bee seemed not to notice the door but continually bumped into the paper windows. People can have many thoughts, but if you tell them not to think this way they will stubbornly continue to do so. At that moment, Gu Ling saw another chance to stir his master's realization, so he said, "Not willing to exit from the open door, you foolishly keep at the windows; sealed with hundred-year-old paper, when will you pop your head through?" In this way, he asked when and how one could become enlightened if he buried his face in ancient scriptures.

The Mind is infinitely flexible. If you do not insist on one particular function, you will not have the corresponding stress. However, stress is created when one insists upon a particular function that is obstructed. If one ignores the open door of emptiness but knocks on the sealed window, stress is created. People do not realize that the nature of the Mind is emptiness. Instead, they rely on a particular function of the Mind in order to deal with stress, much like the bee that continually tries to escape from a sealed window.

A person suffers because the mind is not empty. He is not in control of it, nor will he accept the manifested reality of the moment. Many people cannot change despite all their efforts, because the basis of their thinking is erroneous. Once they let go of reality as they have defined it, the reality will nakedly appear. This is the moment at which the true basis of effort is revealed. However, this does not mean that letting go is all there is. A true letting-go is always followed by a diligent effort to take things up again. When the attachments are gone, reality will manifest so that it can be corrected. Many people lack the ability to change reality, so they misconstrue letting go as a prescription to give up everything and avoid reality. Life will not change for the better unless there is a true emptying of the mind by letting go, followed by proactive engagement with the process of creation. Letting go is about seeing life as a whole, accepting it, finding a solid foothold in reality and then, on that basis, creating changes for a better life.

A wandering Zen monk fell ill during his journey, so he checked into a hostel. In the middle of the night he felt feverish and thirsty, so he groped around in the dark for some water. Coming upon a basin of water, he drank it down and felt much better afterwards. The next morning, he looked for more water to drink and realized what he had drunk during the night was someone's bathwater. He was about to throw up when this thought entered his mind: "Clean and dirty are a state of the mind, having nothing to do with the outside world." This realization is not yet true enlightenment, but it illustrates how the Mind transforms its functions. One day we feel it is dirty, the next day it seems clean. These are the changes of the Mind's function; the perceptions of a person not yet in touch with the source of it all.

Bai Zhang accompanied Master Ma Zu on a walk one day. A flock of wild ducks happened to fly past, so the master asked Bai Zhang, "What are they?" Bai Zhang answered, "Wild ducks." Master Ma Zu then asked, "Where are they now?" Bai Zhang answered, "They have flown away." At this answer, Master Ma Zu turned around and pinched Bai Zhang's nose. As Bai Zhang cried out in pain, Ma Zu said, "You still say they have flown away, huh?" Ma Zu meant that what we see, feel and know comes from ourselves.

Bai Zhang went back to his room in tears, so his fellow monks gathered around and asked if he was missing home or had been scolded by the master. Bai Zhang told them to ask Master Ma Zu, but when they went to the master he said, "Bai Zhang himself knows why. Go ask him." The monks came back and saw Bai Zhang laughing. They were perplexed. "You were just crying. Why are you laughing now?" Bai Zhang replied, "That's right. I was crying, but now I'm laughing." Bai Zhang had not yet become enlightened, but he had come to realize that all appearances are caused by the Mind.

Life is limitless, but ego restricts it, keeping it as a tiny speck that cannot possibly cover the whole world. This kind of life is very limiting, and as a result one finds conflict, suffering and stress everywhere. A person cries when his mind generates a thought to cry, but the Mind itself does not cry. Instead, at any moment it is ready to laugh. This shows how free life can be. One need not be confined within the stress zone. Stress does not come from outside but is actually the result of the ego colliding with the functions of the Mind. The real solution to stress is to dissolve the inner I-consciousness.

Thoughts of worry, due to their nature, will dissolve. The only thing to do is stop perpetuating the same thoughts that give rise to worry. The Mind is infinitely flexible. We do not need to think hard about how to deal with frustration. Instead, simply giving rise to a different thought from your mind will do the trick. In reality, a person will usually go over the same angry or worried thoughts in his or her mind and continually reinforce it. This habit makes the person miserable and stressed, so that he feels there is no choice but to react.

The Mind, by its nature, is free and perfectly at ease in itself. Anything can be placed on an empty tabletop, unless you insist that only a certain thing be placed on it. If your mind is free of egoistic concern, any thought or function can be generated by the Mind. Existence, however, is exclusive. A happy thought naturally dispels a thought of worry; a hand that holds a pen cannot also hold a cup. If the mind is free of seeking or attachment, it is by nature liberated.

Stress occurs when we fail to understand the true nature of our lives and therefore fail to live well. Our true motivation determines how life unfolds. We fail to change life for the better because the real motivating force is the stress created by the disparity between our ego attachment and the wholeness of life's reality. If our reality is already undesirable, why must we push ourselves farther in the same direction? Reducing the disparity automatically reduces stress and gives us a break.

Put your thoughts away so that you can release the stress and experience the real life. Otherwise, your perception of the world will remain a delusion. Everyone has stress, but only self-understanding can lead to the release of that stress. The more we understand who we are, the more we can elevate ourselves. Life's potential is vast and great, so do not limit yourself.

> The bamboo joints show ten years of age;
> A laurel tree emits its fragrance in August.
> Bare branches hold high, beautiful blossoms gone;
> Who is to say that spring is no more?

12 A ZEN TALK ON ALTRUISM

Altruism, righteousness, propriety, wisdom—

These are the Confucian virtues;

Pure Land, Zen, Vinaya, Esoteric—

These are Buddha's compassion.

The Creator alternates spring flowers with the autumn moon;

With compassion, wisdom, aspiration and cultivation,

Bodhisattvas improve on the imperfections of this world.

Use the Resources of Life Instead of Depending on Them

People become religious or spiritual with the intention of opening up new doors in their minds and of having new ideas to guide them onto the path toward a better life. Their daily lives, made up of family, work and chores, are very much driven by habits. Barely any room exists for a new way of thinking about reality. Life's material, however, is like a pond. When the water is stagnant, thoughts and beliefs become putrid. Those who worry keep doing so, while those who are attached and deluded remain as such. So, how do we inject something new into life? We do it by generating more thoughts of kindness and compassion and then seeking a new understanding.

Religious or spiritual groups can guide people toward more kindness and compassion, but ultimately these thoughts can only come from within. They do not come from Buddha, Bodhisattva,

God or any one teacher. If all your problems are due to the failings of others, you may stay home and ignore them because there is nothing you can do. However, if you are the one who created the problems, then you must solve them or they will follow you everywhere. Your behaviors are directed by your thoughts, and these thoughts always accompany you. For example, if you are interested in temples you will most likely visit some when you travel to a foreign country. If you are fond of hot springs, you will look for those instead. Your thoughts will make you do the same thing repeatedly.

New-age philosophy says that man has a mission and a lesson in life. In Buddhism we say, "Everything would be left behind except one's karma." Many groups do not like the concept or karma or do not understand what it is. Karma refers to the state and appearances of life in the present moment, including a person's looks, health and thoughts. Therefore, do not treat karma as something negative. When the state of our life is in distress due to disease or a family dispute, stalled career, poverty or similar circumstances, we call these undesirable conditions and phenomena "obstructive karma." This problem is our lesson, unfinished business or mission. Whether you refer to it as a mission, a lesson or obstructive karma, it is hard to grasp a concept if it has no label. Be careful, however, as labels can be misleading or misused.

The saying, "A man is the product of his environment," demonstrates the human dependence on circumstances. People hypnotize themselves in their environment so that various thoughts are generated, depending on the environment. Even though these thoughts may change, the changes in thought are generally motivated by changes in the environment. For that reason, a person must experience his own "lesson" rather than instantly transcending it.

Naturally, we want to expel frustration and pain when we experience them, but it usually requires that we undergo a long struggle. Imagine that you are upset. Your wife, hoping to console you, might cook a delicious meal. This is a process. Then your child will try to play cute, simply to please you. This is another process. Then you might turn to watching TV in order to calm down. This is yet another step in the process. You learn from a news report that you have just made a gain in the stock market, and as a result you are finally in a good mood. Why does it take so long before you can generate a happy thought and put that bad mood behind you? The more you depend on the surrounding environment, the longer it takes to effect a real change in your emotional state.

Dependency is like a pair of crutches. By nature you do not need them, but if you grow up using crutches, eventually you cannot walk without them. Man can create his own thoughts, environment and relationships; he has limitless potential for creation and self-elevation. However, when he becomes dependent on the phenomena he has created, the relationships and phenomena become his crutches. They are his burden.

Some women love wearing high heels so much that they cannot walk without them. Before high heels, were they able to walk? Yes, of course they were. Then, why can they not now walk without wearing high heels? The answer is that they have become accustomed to them. A person's learning, lesson, karma or mission, whatever you choose to call it, is the result of dependency. If you can master your life, such a crutch will be unnecessary. You do not need a great theory about it, nor do you need people to help you. All that is necessary is the ability to generate one desired thought that makes you happy. You can do this even without a long process of struggle. The longer that struggle is, the more pain it will cause.

No theory, however grand, can surpass the reality of life. Therefore, understanding your life is far more important than knowing any religion. All theories of religious, spiritual or psychological growth serve the purpose of elevating humanity. They are like ingredients for cooking. If you, the chef, make good use of the ingredients, you will cook up a beautiful life.

Recognize the Symptoms and Cease Your Misguided Efforts

Why do most people who search for happiness fail to find it despite their serious efforts? It is because such efforts are misguided. Undesirable situations in a person's life serve as indicators of misguided efforts that need correction. Looking at a handful of seeds, you probably cannot tell the good ones from the bad ones. Similarly, you probably cannot foresee the kind of reality that will manifest in response to your thoughts. You should at least know who you are and the reality you have right now, so that you can discern the kinds of thoughts that lead to this reality. If you see an orange on a tree, is it not be obvious what kind of seed was planted?

Frustration, troubles, unpleasant looks, poor relationships or the shortage of money: the appearances of these obstructive karmas point out what kind of attitude adjustment must be made within the mind. You are not a saint, so you might not foresee the consequences a particular thought will cause in the long run, but at least your eyes and ears can identify the sour oranges. Self-pity is a sour orange, a lack of money is a sour orange, and poor relationships are sour oranges. What can be done?

Ours is a fast-food society in which people want instant change. A student asked for my opinion on the war in Iraq. I replied, "When I become the President, I will be in the position to decide whether to increase troops or to withdraw. As for now, my position is in the lecture hall to share my teaching with everyone." The student then asked me how to achieve world peace. I said, "When you meditate well, the world will be peaceful." He then asked, "Is meditation not too passive?" The quality of being passive or active is a relative concept, and inappropriate activity can be even more passive.

Some places get lots of snow in winter. The Chinese saying that "cleaning snow in front of one's own door, never mind the frost on others' roofs" is typically a negative statement about selfishness. However, if everyone shovels the snow in front of his or her own house, there will be no obstruction anywhere. Taking care of our own business is actually a very positive thing. Can I generate thoughts for you? I cannot. I can teach you how to generate thoughts, but it is still up to you to do so. Someone may help you shovel the snow now, but what will happen when it snows again? You can depend upon your parents or children, but what if the person you depend upon dies? However great or sensible an idea might be, a person has to think of it and then apply it. "Cleaning snow in front of one's own house" is actually a compassionate concept that should be propagated far and wide. "You can lead the cow to the river, but you cannot make it drink." I cannot help you to be happy. Only you can make that happen.

Everyone wants happiness. How many ways have you tried to reach that goal? Many people rush to those "how to be happy, healthy and rich" seminars and try all sorts of methods that "guarantee" happiness. Do they really work? The real guarantee for the desired result is based on the right understanding, which is like the seed. If you plant the wrong seed, inevitably you will harvest the wrong fruit.

What are your thoughts? Who are you? What is the foundation of your life? What are the predicaments in your life right now? Talking about life change before finding answers to these questions means you are like a blindfolded man who is clueless to his whereabouts but tries hard to go to some particular place. If you do not know where you are and what your reality is, all your efforts will be in vain. If you are certain of your exact position, every step will be real. Progress may seem slow, but it is solid.

Today there are many issues in regard to parenting. As parents, your state of mind depends on a certain environment. Children's minds also have certain dependencies on their environment. Because of the differences in the environment, which changes over time, a generation gap exists between the parents' and children's states of mind, and gaps emerge between parents and children. Dependency on different surroundings leads to differences in mentality, or the so-called "gap." Because we are dependent upon the environment, our state of mind is shaped accordingly. For example, if a pregnant woman gets into frequent disputes, her newborn baby will have a disturbed mentality. If she meditates frequently, her newborn will develop a calm, stable mind in reflection of the environment.

"One more share of effort beforehand, one less share of worry afterwards": This is the way life is. Do not wait until problems arise before you act. Once problems occur, considerable time and effort are needed to solve them. Do not wait for disease to strike, because once you are sick it is a long road to recovery. However, people usually do not work at getting to know themselves until issues accumulate around them. The symptoms of a disease are actually the accumulated energy of negative thoughts, as described in the Buddhist concept of aggregation in the Four Noble Truths. Here, aggregation is the cause of suffering.

How many thoughts do we have from morning to evening? There are many. Among all the thoughts we have in a single day, of how many are we aware? What happened today? How many of those thoughts can you recall? We can remember just a few. People usually are not aware of ninety-nine percent of their thoughts, but every thought has an impact on the thinker's life. A happy thought makes you smile and feel good because it can also affect your hormones, but an angry thought makes you uncomfortable. You get sick because you do not know your thoughts. When we become ill, there is the symptom, but the causes—the accumulation of negative energy—already started to accumulate before the symptoms were evident. In modern terminology, we call the cause of illness the accumulation of energy. In Buddhism, it is referred to as the aggregation. Aggregation means stagnation, indigestion and unfinished actions. Accordingly, it means we have not functioned through means of the "mind without abiding." Instead, we have held onto a thought we created.

If you are heavily dependent upon the external, you cannot reveal the pure nature of the Mind. The Mind is a container without boundaries, but if you continue to put the wrong things in it until they accumulate and become stagnant, eventually they will become the causes of disease. A rigid mind reacts to different environments with the same mentality, and therefore it is impossible to accumulate positive energy. There is no guarantee that we can attain happiness this way. Ignorant of our own thinking, we live our lives as if we are walking in the air, with no foundation underneath and no certainty of outcome.

You are committed to your opinions, and others are committed to theirs. In reality, you have no choice but to stick to your own ideas. Also, your children hold to their respective positions: What you want is not what they want and vice versa. When opinions differ, fights occur. If we fail to deal with dualistic thinking, war will be inevitable. Sometimes a person is even at war with himself. For example, imagine that you love diamonds. You look for them as you shop. You feel sad if you do not buy one, but you feel guilty if you do. When you do buy one, you feel obliged to return it because the diamond is not truly necessary. Torn among these wants and "want-nots," and the "shoulds" and "should-nots," you are at war with your own mind. You may even tell yourself that since you are practicing Buddhism and spiritual growth, such conflicts and vexations should not occur. Nevertheless, conflicts continue to arise in your reality. The fact is, what should not happen already has. To dwell on these dualities is to create war.

The capacity of the Mind is unlimited, because its nature is emptiness. Unfortunately, this unbounded, vast nature of the Mind has been blocked by rigid thought patterns and personalities. Man uses his mind to give rise to energy that accumulates into symptoms of illness. When relationship and health problems start to manifest, they are simply the tip of the iceberg. In fact, the underlying reality has accumulated for a long time. Disease, poor relationships and unpleasant looks are all the products of incorrect, negative ways of using the mind. These symptoms indicate a kind of fragmentation within the mind of the sufferer.

Appearances come from the Mind, and consequently your looks reflect your inner state. For instance, a person who is not good-looking can be pleasant and beautiful if he or she is happy. When the symptoms of disease manifest, they cannot be dealt with hastily, because efforts in the wrong direction can do more harm than good. When we are faced with obstructive karma, it is time to look within and see what the real lesson is. Our karma, lesson or mission is already here, so the important thing is to see it and dissolve the obstructions. The more dependent on the external environment we become, the less creativity we will have and the more frustration we will experience. Although no one wants to be overly dependent and rigid, most people are.

Dispel Dualism: Love Others and Love Yourself

A holistic, harmonious mind is free of dualism. A happy thought is different from an angry thought, but they are created by the same Mind. If you can find this source, you can also tap its unlimited creativity. People usually identify with an angry thought as their complete self, forgetting that this thought was just a creation of the Mind. By identifying yourself with your thoughts, you will live in dualism and its ups and downs. You will not be able to free yourself and recognize the absolute, non-dualistic Mind.

Master Wen Yi ran into Master Gui Chen, whereupon they engaged in a discussion of the concept, "I and the universe have the same root." Gui Chen asked Wen Yi, "You and the universe have the same root, so are you and the universe the same thing?" Wen Yi replied, "No. We are not the same thing." Hearing this, Gui Chen extended two fingers to Wen Yi. Seeing the two fingers, Wen Yi immediately changed and said instead, "Yes, we are the same."

If I extend two fingers now, would you think it means one or two? If you say two, you overlooked one, but if you say one, you ignored two. If you say neither one nor two, you have not seen anything, but if you say both one and two, your vision is blurred. If you get it, it means you are enlightened: This is a matter of reality. However, if you think "scissors" when I extend two fingers, it means your mind is not free. Instead, your mind is generating thoughts out of dependence on the external, being the scissors in this case. So, is it one or two, or is it scissors? One either knows or does not know.

"The universe and I have the same root." It is neither one nor two, and it is both one and two. To know does not mean knowing the answer; instead, it means knowing your life. Who makes you see and think? What is happening in your life right now? Pay attention here. It is your life that is happening right now, not something outside it. The key to dispelling dualism lies in the understanding that life is a whole without inner and outer distinctions. However, to dispel dualism is not to deny its presence. Buddhist teaching defines this as "neither together nor separate; neither one nor two; the whole is the individual, but among the individual there are differences." There is sameness in differences, but this sameness manifests differences; neither dualistic nor non-dualistic, with neither negation nor independence.

A mind that is free of dualism is calm and free of dependency. A dependent mind is neither calm nor in charge of itself. Instead, its thoughts are trapped in a circle that will drag down the person's learning process in life. You must constantly dissolve the energy of every creation into emptiness. Emptiness is not nothingness but is integration into the essence. This is what is meant by "no abiding" in the sutra statement about "generating the mind with no abiding." You have to let go. You cannot abide in anything, because every phenomenon disappears the moment it manifests.

It is superstitious to follow without understanding; any action should be preceded by understanding. You must truly understand this universal principle. The principle of "no abiding," for example, is a must. It is not simply the reality of the historical Buddha but it is the principle that governs the reality of all beings. Your thoughts change constantly from moment to moment. Can you hold onto any of them? Even the thought of holding onto a thought can change! Likewise, your body and relationships are ever-changing. To which do you hold?

According to the teaching of impermanence, you will die and

all you have in this life will part from you: your children, your money and all your belongings. It may sound depressing, but this is the truth, and truth is neither pessimistic nor optimistic. People, due to their expectations, feel pessimistic when you tell them that what they expect will ultimately go away. However, from a different perspective, impermanence is what enables you to change for the better. You cannot be better than you already are if everything is fixed permanently. Change shows the proactive side of life's creative capacity. Your desire for better health can only be fulfilled through change. If nothing ever changes, what fun is left in life?

The stability that humans seek is only an illusion. None of us can be happy if nothing ever changes. You should not fear death but instead should fear the failure to die, because this is what goes with you forever. Because the ability of the Mind is everlasting—and because it is not energy itself but the creator of energy—the body dies and the Mind continues to exist. The Mind, which is formless, is not within the five elements, but it can create the five elements. This Mind, the source of life, is by nature Nirvana. It is the Pure Land and Pure Bliss. This Mind is always here, and it will not die. Therefore, you have no choice but to learn to live with it in harmony.

Your ability to generate thoughts is miraculous, but because you will suffer it is also a kind of obstructive karma. If you know how to use it, you will enjoy happiness in life. Therefore, do not worry about death, because the real concern is how to live. Death is already evident: Is not the ten-year-old you dead? What can you ever keep? Nothing. Death is in every moment, so there is no need to worry. Instead, worry about how to live better in each moment of your life.

Inner peace requires that you should not always be so insistent. If you know your insistence today may become tomorrow's regret, then you will not be so stubborn. Some degree of persistence is needed for any creative endeavor, but the damage of insistence on the wrong things is hard to repair. Do not see life as good or bad, as if it were only black and white. The truth is that good and bad coexist within the confines of life. Therefore, Buddhist teachings describe this world as "bearable," in which people must bear their spouses, parents, children, bosses, colleagues, salaries, traffic jams and so forth. We all live our life by bearing through it. This is a fact.

To love others and love yourself, you must first identify dualism and eliminate it. If you cannot get back into the pure, blissful, empty nature of the Mind, you will not dissolve and integrate the energy of your dualistic creations. If you create and accumulate undigested energy day in and day out, inevitably you will develop health or relationship issues. All forms of obstacles—in terms of personality, beliefs, health and relationships—result from the accumulation of unwholesome energy. In other words, the obstacles are created by the lack of skillfulness in using the Mind to create the desired outcome. It has created too many negative side effects.

Create the reality you want, and subsequently you can return it to equanimity. A disciple of mine went to Mainland China for a visit to temples. Upon his return, he said he had thought of me while reading a verse in a temple, "When you see it, do it; after you do it, let it go. Having let go, how can there be anything unfinished?" The principle in this verse should be practiced. Here is a piece of ancient wisdom that is beyond time and space. It is applicable even now. Those who are wise know they must live their lives according to the truth of the universe.

The wise man does not look for wisdom. Instead, he discovers the wisdom that is already in his mind. The Mind is by nature pure and free, so there is no need to seek elsewhere. The only task for us is to discover it, understand it and live in it. The nature and capacity of the Mind are the same for all, without exception. The wise man simply manifests and lives his life accordingly. Everything you need is already in you, but you simply do not recognize it or use it correctly. It takes practice to do so.

Use Your Thoughts to Achieve Your Goals

A calm mind is flexible and alert. It knows what you and others want, and it knows when to act. You possess limitless potential for creation, so do not obsess over any particular creation. If it is not working properly, set it aside. Life should begin by setting a clear goal, which must be followed by the skillful use of methods. Imagine that your wife is upset with you. You buy flowers and gifts to soothe her, hoping to keep the peace, but she refuses to be pleased. In this situation, you might feel inclined to say, "I've bought flowers and apologized, so what else do you expect me to do?" Here you have already failed in the first step, and therefore you have failed with respect to the goal. Are you trying to insist on your way, or are you trying to reach the goal?

People often insist on their approach instead of the goal, but ultimately that kind of aggressive action will fail. You should choose an approach for the sake of reaching the goal. If your wife is still upset, why not smile and ask her whether she would like you to cook dinner tonight? You may not need to actually cook, because once your wife is happy she will likely be glad to fix dinner for you. So, identify your goal and use different tools to reach it. If you fail, it is still a failure regardless of which tool you used.

You are more than the sum of your thoughts and emotions. You have potential for unlimited creation and growth, but you must employ the right tools. Persistence alone cannot do the job. Instead, it takes the right idea and action to reach your destination. Therefore, always reflect on whether your attitude and ideas can lead you toward the goal. If not, why not let it go? Of course, if the intended destination is wrong to begin with, by fair means or by foul, you will not attain the desired outcome.

A mind that is calm and agile lives harmoniously with everyone. A calm mind and abidance in peace with each individual are the foundation for a good family, good neighborhood, good society, good country and a peaceful world. World peace is an ancient and ongoing topic, but how do we achieve it? World peace starts with each peaceful mind. Slogans for world peace from disturbed minds are nothing more than noise and jokes.

True world peace cannot be achieved unless every mind is calm and peaceful. Only when each individual keeps his mind at peace will it be possible to talk about world peace. Therefore, world peace starts with meditation and inner reflection, not simply aggressive pursuit. Aggressive pursuit along the wrong direction can only lead us away from the goal. The right cause guarantees the production of the right fruit, even if the process takes time.

Start with meditation, which cultivates and calms the mind and keeps it under control. Do it with slow but steady effort. Meditation may at first seem irrelevant to the state of economic crisis or ethnic conflict, but it is in fact the only guarantee to solving issues ranging from the Iraq War to personal disputes. Calm the mind—free the mind—and life will indeed be wholesome.

Beyond the sky there is more sky;

Beside a great man there are still greater men.

After each thought, endless thoughts follow;

Inside the void there is a void that negates void-ness.

13 THE TRUTH SURPASSES ALL

Wei Tuo, the Lokapala, protects the dharma everywhere;

His sincere mind hears every corner.

People across the five continents all have Buddha nature;

As long as they cultivate its root, wisdom will arrive.

Multifaceted Society, Universal Truth

Some may wonder why Western societies worship God but not Buddha, or why the Eastern societies worship Buddha but not God. This is similar to asking why the Eskimos live near the Arctic Pole or why cacti grow in the desert. There could be many cultural or scientific explanations for these phenomena, but from a Buddhist perspective everything is a dependently arising manifestation of shared karma originating from the Mind. Any phenomenon results from the confluence of various conditions. Any form of existence is due to the aggregation of factors. In Buddhism, we say "based on cause, through conditions," meaning that the environment and our cultural background are creations of the shared karma of individuals with similar mind functions. So are the religions of Buddhism, Christianity and Islam. It is not the case that religion causes certain shared karma. Instead, religion is simply a karmic aspect of the shared karma of the Collective.

Regardless of the different interpretations on the concept of God as the Creator of man, the formless, omnipotent and omnipresent nature of God is very similar to the idea of Buddha nature or the Primordial Mind of Zen.

According to Buddhism, everyone can become a Buddha. The relationship between the metaphysical Mind and the physical human is that of essence and function. Our various "selves," in different times and spaces, are simply different aspects of the Mind. There is not a primary-versus-secondary relationship between independently self-existing manifestations and the essence. Even the Buddha statue that people worship is no more than a manifested form of the formless Buddha nature. Similarly, this applies to all living creatures: Their essence is also the formless Buddha nature. The source of life has neither shape nor form, but it is innate to all beings. Any existence in a particular time and space is simply due to the functioning of the Mind in the moment.

The ancients said, "Karmic manifestation is not real; ungraspable; Buddha nature is pure and boundless. In a thousand rivers there are a thousand moon reflections; a ten-thousand-mile sky is cloudless." The reflections of a thousand different moons in a thousand rivers appear in accordance with the ripening of conditions of the Mind's functioning, and instantly vanish as the direction and conditions of the Mind's functioning change. Likewise, the function of the Mind creates different manifestations through the Buddha Nature. Every existence is momentary; existence and emptiness are simultaneous and inseparable aspects of phenomena. Every moment in the existence of an ordinary human being results from the subconscious function of the Mind, which drifts according to the flow of ever-changing conditions. People grasp these momentary phenomena and develop the illusion that there is an actual "I." The force of this phenomenon-grasping tendency takes the appearances of the Mind as independent, substantive existences. Having become ignorant of the innate Mind, which is the source of life, we drift with those phenomena.

The anthropomorphic conceptualization of God, however, changes the relationship between God and man into a primary-versus-secondary relationship involving two isolated entities. In this relationship, the metaphysical God and the physical manifestations thereof exist independently, so what is human can never become God. This conception leads believers to focus on developing phenomena. If you were to see the physical appearance of God, you would then ask yourself how an omnipresent being could appear in front of you. A physical existence can only exist within the limits of time and space; it cannot be omnipresent. Only a true Self or God that is devoid of "I" can possibly be omnipresent in all appearances.

All appearances are the corresponding results of the functions of the Mind or Buddha nature. Appearances of ordinary beings and the Buddha are both subject to the impermanence of conditioned changes. The Diamond Sutra says, "When one sees through all appearances as unreal, one sees Buddha." Through the appearances of Buddha, the creative force behind all phenomena that is the real Buddha can be recognized. Thus the Mind, which is formless, exists for all time.

The reason people are reluctant to accept Buddha dharma is because they consider Buddhism just another religion. They see no reason to leave one religion simply to enter another. Moreover, they see that some Buddhists claim Buddhism as the one and only truth, just as they see adherents to other religions do. We must seek to understand the truth from a holistic perspective in order to avoid the extreme of self-righteous prejudice. What we perceive as Buddhism today is just a particular approach to implementing the truth that Sakyamuni discovered. It is this formalized approach that has become a religion.

Truth did not become truth with the birth of the founder of a religion. Truth is everlasting and universal, transcending history, religions, cultures, races and societies. The East and the West have different cultures, but the principle governing the way of their cultures is the same. The search for truth is a common quest of all humanity, and a truth-seeking mind will eventually lead the person who uses it to the universal truth.

The pursuit of happiness and immortality is as ancient as human history. Everything in life is impermanent, and consequently man has no choice but to find a refuge for his life in this ever-changing world. This is a fact of our existence. All beings experience suffering and pain; every household has a tough book to read. People, solely through the use of this primordial Mind, create their own karma and must take responsibility for the consequences thereof. Religion should support the universal experience of the struggle of humanity without becoming a process of imposing one culture onto another. Each religion is the karmic consequence of the shared karma unique to each group, and therefore it is uniquely suitable only to that group. The core of Buddha's teaching is how to eradicate attachment in order to live life with greater flexibility; how to cope with the impermanent nature of life and stay away from misery; how to manifest the pure mind and reach freedom; and how to use the Mind to create happiness.

All existence must return, from its present standpoint, to the source from which it came. Thus the followers of the Theravada sect do not necessarily require Mahayana Buddhism in order to attain liberation. Similarly, a Mahayana practitioner does not necessarily require an Esoteric method in order to be free. What must be understood is the common principle that governs the emergence of the various sects; that is, each sect is a mind-creation dependently arising from karma. Thus it comes, and thus it goes. The foundation of all sects is the universal truth, which is practiced in ways that are suited to the local culture, history and social development. However, the concept underlying the practice is the same: The Mind is innate to all, whether one is in the East or the West. The elimination of attachment will reveal the primordial emptiness and liberation, which are inherent to the Mind. The application of this universal truth, of the primordial Mind Essence, will accomplish the spirit of benefiting all beings and ultimately attain freedom.

The universal concepts of equality, egoless integration and universal compassion that embrace diversity are most suitable in a multicultural society. Only universal concepts can adapt to a society that is multifaceted and rapidly developing. Only a universal concept can be applied in the spirit of equality, egoless integration and universal compassion that embraces all ethnic and cultural differences so that the beauty of diversity can blossom.

Modern-day people will generally perceive of Zen as liberation and ease of self. Given the pursuit of freedom, they become interested in ease of self and tend to characterize the idea of liberation or Nirvana as an ancient, mysterious thing. However, we must familiarize ourselves with the connection between ritual practices and individual liberation. Thus we can recognize that all rituals are simply methods for the self-control and introspection that ultimately lead to the realization of the nature of the Mind and its creative power. Nowadays, many Buddhist ritual practices have been secularized in a way that deviates from the spiritual essence and causes them to become ineffective while leading many to assume that Buddhism is a superstition.

Apply the Universal Truth, Just Use This Mind; Just Use This Mind to Apply the Universal Truth

Spirituality starts with the establishment of the right understanding. Ineffectiveness in spiritual practice is due to misunderstanding of the concept and methods as well as the goal of the methods. Right now, many people accept meditation with great interest but are more hesitant about the concept of reincarnation. In reality, the practice that is directly rooted in the present is the most proactive means of dealing with the issue of reincarnation, because all anyone can really control is the present. Therefore, it is best for you to learn to face the present, work with the present and elevate the present with a calm mind, regardless whether you accept the idea of reincarnation. The common interpretation of reincarnation is also based on convenience, in which the past, present and future are treated as a linear concept. Life, however, is not a linear development. Instead, it is the holistic unfolding of countless conditions whereby each moment is simply a different functional focal point.

Only universal truth can endure the test of time, space and ever-changing conditions; only universal truth can elevate life and reveal the light of the Mind. Universal truth transcends rationality and sensibility, good and evil, shape and form, race and religion; it cannot be owned by any one person. Because universal truth can benefit all sentient beings, we must promote it. We hope the concept of the Mind's innate wisdom and compassion can take root in this modern age, so that all human beings with dharma connection to the teaching will accept and take it to heart and diligently practice with the goal of elevating human society and manifesting a better reality on earth.

All forms of existence, from a land of defilement to wholeness, result from different levels of mind purification. From an ordinary being to arahant, bodhisattva and eventually Buddhahood, these are the evolutionary roles we play in spiritual practice. Every corner of the world should hear the principles of cultivating the universal truth of the Mind. From now till eternity, it is my wish that every person will know that he is the master of his own reality and will practice for the sake of his happiness and perfection. This is my goal.

Most people insist that the doctrines of their beliefs are superior to others. However, every individual lives in a world in which he alone exists. There is no need to worry about why his world is such, because everyone has his share of the universe. What we should instead focus on is whether we have done our best in this world.

Who I am determines who will be around me. If you elevate yourself, your karma will follow. This is the unchanging truth. Someone once asked me, "Should a person set a plan in life or just be at peace and go with the flow?" I say that you should have a plan as you follow the flow. A plan sets a goal or an ideal that may not be achievable. Therefore, once you set a plan and endeavor accordingly, you should be flexible enough to adjust with the flow of life. A plan is a goal, but it is also a process because life is an eternal effort.

We should strive, as we transcend cultural barriers, to reveal the nature of the Mind and adopt the concept of universal compassion, equanimity and the understanding of the nature of the Mind. Such altruism is essential in order to establish a better reality in the here-and-now, which will benefit all beings and society as a whole.

Universal truth transcends cultural structures and religious rituals and rules. Even though some cultural background and religious ritual and rules are necessary in teaching dharma, one must not be limited by them or let them hinder the truth. A practitioner is not here to learn the rituals and rules, the preacher's culture or even the religion; these things are not the essence. What he needs to walk away with is the understanding of the Mind. Only through the direct experience of the Mind's nature can you find eternal freedom in life.

The realization of life's essence is to practice according to the universal truth. All beings possess this innate Mind. Whether ignorant or enlightened, ordinary or saintly, a reincarnation or a perfected immortality, there is nothing to do but "Just Use This Mind." This is the universal truth.

The Mind is not lesser for the ordinary, nor is it greater for the enlightened. The Mind is the same in the East as in the West, in ancient times and modern times, for all beings. "Just Use This Mind" is how all sentient beings create, manifest, handle and live with their karmas.

To apply the universal truth, just use this mind. Just use this Mind to apply the universal truth. The guiding principle of my teaching is to promote the concept of non-duality to all. I believe there will be results, as long as I try.

We have reached the last page of the book. At this point, how many are asleep, and how many are awake?

Remote hills, covered with planted pines;

woodmen everywhere.

You have your house, I have mine;

each worships his own ancestors.

Five hundred years ago we were originally one clan;

today only hostility and suspicion remain.

Mid-autumn Festival is historical; even

Persia celebrated it with music and dance.

No need to fight, no need to pursue;

half a verse is your ticket to the West Paradise.

Under the starry night and bright moon,

houses lit up and flowers in their yards.

Leaning on a rock and smiling, I have the moon all to myself;

who would have thought, everywhere I go

flowers and the moon follow.

Listen carefully but do not speak;

Flowing spring stirs up silent waves without intent,

big and small bubbles with countless colors.

Countless colors, countless forms

Any one of them I take with me and cherish it.

Cherish it, stay with you

The Goddess Chang'e escapes to the moon.

Take care, each and every one!

GLOSSARY

GLOSSARY

AMIDA BUDDHA: The *Amida Buddha,* also known as *Amitabha Buddha* or *Amitayus Buddha,* is the root teacher of the Western Land of Bliss. *Amida* means Infinity. *Amitabha* and *Amitayus* mean Infinite Light (Space) and Infinite Life (Time), respectively.

AMITBHA BUDDHA: See Amida Buddha.

AMITABHA SUTRA: The *Amitabha Sutra* is a scriptural text that describes the aspirations and miraculous manifestations of the Western Land of Bliss of Amitabha Buddha.

ARAHANT: An *arahant* is one who has attained a spiritual state of liberation in which habitual tendencies, such as defining and clinging to the notion of "I," have been purified to the point that the individual is free from life after life of reincarnation.

ATTACHMENT: *Attachment* is a state of mind characterized by grasping or holding onto mental functions, such as thoughts, feelings and perceptions. The most fundamental attachment human beings have is to their sense of an independent selfhood.

AVATAMSAKA SUTRA: Also known as Hua-Yen in Chinese, this sutra teaches the simultaneity and totality of the manifestation of phenomena. It shows the integral relationship between phenomena and the ultimate principle, and the essential non-difference of phenomena.

MASTER BAI-ZHANG: *Master Bai-Zhang Huai-Hai* (720 - 814), the teacher of Huang-Bo, was instrumental in reforming and establishing the rules that governed how Zen practitioners should live and practice together as a self-sustaining community where, in addition to meditation, manual labor for farming and upkeep of the monastery became an integral part of Zen practice. The event that was the precursor to his enlightenment went like this: One time he was attending to Master Ma-tzu and a flock of wild geese flew by. Ma-tzu asked him, "What is it?" Bai-zhang replied, "Wild geese." Ma-tzu then asked, "Where did it go?" Bai-zhang said, "They flew away." Without warning, Ma-tzu turned around and got a hold of Bai-zhang's nose and twisted hard. Bai-zhang cried out in pain, and Ma-tzu said, "And you told me it flew away!?" At this instant, Bai-zhang had some realization. Returning to his quarters, Bai-zhang began crying and a fellow monk asked him, "Are you missing your folks?" No. "Did you get scolded by the teacher?" No. "Then why are you crying?" Bai-zhang said, "My nose was twisted by Master and the pain did not quite penetrate through!" The other monk then asked, "What is not working out?" Bai-zhang said, "Go ask the master himself." When the monk asked the master about the situation, Ma-tzu said, "He [Bai-zhang] knows it, go ask him!" When the monk returned, Bai-zhang was laughing out loud! Puzzled, he said, "Bai-zhang, you were just crying, why is it you are now laughing so hard?" Bai-zhang said, "Was just crying, now laughing." The monk was still puzzled. Later on Bai-zhang achieved a further breakthrough and his realization was confirmed by Ma-tzu.

BARDO: *Bardo* is the transitional state between successive incarnation. It typically refers to what occurs after the death of the physical body but before the being takes rebirth in one of the six possible realms.

BODHI: *Bodhi* is a Sanskrit word meaning awakening.

BODHICITTA: *Bodhicitta* means the awakening mind, the fundamental awakening nature that is innate in all sentient beings.

BODHI TREE: The *Bodhi Tree* is the sacred fig tree in Bodh Gaya, India, under which the historical Buddha attained enlightenment.

BODHISATTVA: A *bodhisattva* is a practitioner—either in the process of attaining or having already attained a high-level of spiritual awakening and freedom from suffering—who strives to help others achieve the same state. This altruistic action is based on the profound recognition of the inseparability of the personal self and others. The term *bodhisattva* also represents the myriad pure functions that arise from the Pure Mind.

BODHI TAO: *Tao* is Chinese meaning the "Way." Bodhi Tao refers to the principle of how the Mind functions.

BUDDHA DHARMA: The teaching of the Buddha.

BUDDHA NATURE: The fundamental nature of the Mind that is innate in all beings. Because of this fundamental equality in the nature of the Mind, all beings have the potential for awakening.

BUDDHAHOOD: *Buddhahood* is the spiritual state of complete liberation from suffering and the perfection of all virtues. It is the state of complete realization of the essence of the Mind and the perfection of the Mind's functions.

CAOXI: The *Caoxi* is a river in Southern China where the Zen teaching of the Sixth Patriarch began. *Caoxi* also refers to the Zen lineage and its teaching that can be traced to the Sixth Patriarch.

CHANG'E (GODDESS) : *Chang'e* is the deity of the Moon in ancient Chinese mythology.

CITTAMATRA: *Cittamatra* is a school of Buddhism based on the "mind-only" philosophy.

COLLECTIVE (THE): The *Collective* refers to the totality of all manifestations of the Mind.

CONFUCIUS: See Confucianism.

CONFUCIANISM: *Confucianism* is a set of ethical doctrines preached by Confucius (551 - 478 BCE) that has been highly influential in China. *Confucianism* stresses the importance of proper conduct and responsibility in the context of relationships, such as the relationship between rulers and the ruled, father and son, husband and wife, elders and the young, and between friends. It is a humanistic ethical system not based on any theistic belief.

DA-YU: *DaYu* is a mountain in southern China where the Sixth Patriarch gave his first teaching to a spiritual seeker after attaining enlightenment.

DAO: (or Tao) Also referred to as "The Way," *Tao* refers to the principle that governs the functioning of the Mind and reality.

DAOISM: (or Taoism) *Taoism* is a set of philosophical teachings and religious practices that originated in China and became an organized religion in the fifth century AD. The key text in Taoism is the *Tao Te Ching*. Taoists believe that man should live in harmony with nature through the Tao or "the Way," the idea of a great cosmic harmony. Taoist beliefs emphasize self-refinement, liberty and the pursuit of immortality.

DEVA: *Deva* is a non-human being that possesses greater power and whose mind strongly exhibits the qualities of kindness, compassion, sympathetic joy and equanimity.

DHARMA: *Dharma* literally means law, rule or duty. It may refer to the Buddhist teaching or to the ultimate truth being expressed by the teaching. In Buddhist philosophy, dharma also refers to phenomenon.

DIAMOND SUTRA: The *Diamond Sutra* is a Mahayana Sutra, based on a dialogue between the Buddha and his disciple Subhuti, which focuses on the practice of overcoming dualism and attachment to forms.

MASTER DONG SHAN: *Master Dong Shan* (807 - 869) was the co-founder of the Caodong (or "Soto" in Japanese) school of Zen that focuses on the practice of Silent Illumination as a way of realizing the nature of the Mind.

DUALISM: *Dualism* is a philosophy or approach characterized by the separation opposites of mutually dependent parts such as subject and object, self and others, good and evil, etc.

EGOLESSNESS: *Egolessness* is one of the core teachings of the Buddha. It points out the illusion of "I" or ego-identification.

EIGHTY-EIGHT BUDDHAS REPENTANCE: The *Eighty-eight Buddhas Repentance* is a ritual practice of confessing, repenting, and resolving to abstain from harmful actions. During the ritual, Eighty-eight Buddhas' names were chanted, in combination with prostration to pacify the practitioner's normally restless and egocentric mind so that a state of mental clarity and repentance can arise.

EIGHT IMMORTALS: The *Eight Immortals* are eight legendary "saints" in the Daoist religion who have attain the state of immortality.

ELDER ZHAOZHOU: *Zhaozhou,* or Chao-Chou ("Joshu" in Japanese) was one of the most famous Chinese Zen Masters in the Tang Dynasty (618 - 907 AD). Chao-Chou is widely known for the classic *koan* where in response to the question of whether a dog possesses the Buddha Nature—the potential for awakening—he uttered the word "Wu" (or "Mu" in Japanese), which is often incorporated into the practice of Zen inquiry.

ENLIGHTMENT: *Enlightment* is the recognition of the nature of the Mind.

EMPTINESS: The word *Emptiness* refers to the lack of intrinsic existence of any phenomena.

ESOTERIC: See Vajrayana.

FIFTH PATRIARCH HONG REN: The *Fifth Patriarch Hong Ren* (601 - 674) taught the Diamond Sutra to the Sixth Patriarch, which led to his awakening.

FIVE COMMANDMENTS AND THE TEN GOOD ACTIONS: The *Five Commandments and the Ten Good Actions* are the five precepts of a lay Buddhist practitioner, namely, no killing, no stealing, no wrongful sexual conduct, no falsehood in speech, no intoxicants. The ten good actions are typically stated as negation: no killing, no stealing, no wrongful sexual conduct, no abusive speech, no seductive speech, no divisive speech, no lies, no greed, no hatred, no delusion.

FIVE PLATFORM: *Five Platform* or Five Plateaus (WuTai), is a sacred mountain in Chinese Buddhism. It is legendary for many manifestations of the teaching and activities attributed to the Bodhisattva of Wisdom (Manjushri).

FOUR NOBLE TRUTHS: The first sermon taught by the historical Buddha, the *Four Noble Truths* are: (1) the nature of suffering, (2) the cause of suffering is attachment, (3) suffering ceases when attachment is removed, and (4) the way to remove attachment is through proper cultivation of the eight aspects of our life: understanding (or view) of reality, thought, speech, action, livelihood, effort, attention and mental concentration.

FOURTH ZEN PATRIARCH DAO XIN: Zen patriarchs are considered the orthodox line of transmission of Zen teaching, the embodiment of the direct realization of the truth rather than mere intellectual understanding or written words. The Fourth Patriarch in China, recognized as having attained this direct realization of the truth, was *Dao Xin* (580 - 651 AD).

FAHUA SUTRA: Also known as the Lotus Sutra. Among many of the *Fahua Sutra* key teachings is that while the Buddha has taught many different practices to suit the needs of various practitioners, ultimately there is only one vehicle to enlightenment: the vehicle of Awakening. Also in the sutra, the Buddha stressed that all beings have the potential for Awakening.

GANGES: The *Ganges* is a sacred river in India.

GUANG QIN: Master *Guang Qin (*1892 - 1986*)*, though illiterate, was highly revered for his spiritual realization and his Pure Land teaching. Just before passing away, he said, "No coming, no going, nothing happened."

MASTER GUI SHAN: *Master Gui Shan* (771 - 853) was a founder of the GuiYan school of Zen.

HUA-YEN: In Chinese *Hua-Yen* means Flower Garlands. A school of Buddhism that emerged in the sixth century in China, based on the teaching of the Flower Garland Sutra.

HUA-TOU PRACTICE: The continuous and intensive questioning of a Zen story as crystallized by a single phrase or a single word such as "Wu" (or Mu in Japanese) or "What is the meaning of Bodhidharma's coming from the West?" or "Who is the one reciting the Buddha's Name?" The purpose of the *Huatou practice* is to utilize the doubt generated by the questioning to penetrate through our habitual attachments and directly experience the nature of the pure mind.

MASTER HUI NENG: Sixth Patriarch *Hui-Neng* (638 - 713 BCE), regarded as the most important figure in Zen Buddhism, was instrumental in the wide propagation of Zen practice in China and later in Japan and Korea. All five schools of Zen Buddhism can trace their lineage to *Hui-Neng*. His teaching, as recorded in the Platform Sutra, is the most important source of early Zen teaching.

HUI ZHONG (IMPERIAL PRECEPTOR): (675 - 775) National Teacher *Hui Zhong*, of the Tang Dynasty, was a disciple of the Sixth Patriarch Hui-Neng and attained enlightenment under his guidance. After awakening to the Way, he went into retreat in the Dan-Tzi Valley of White Cliff Mountain for forty years. Emperor Xu Zung knew of his attainment and invited him to be the national teacher.

INVASION OF THE FIVE BARBARIANS: The *Invasion of the Five Barbarians* was a period of political chaos in China due to the invasion of five nomadic tribes. The Chinese term for Barbarian is "Hu," meaning foreigner—not always a negative term but implying a lack of culture or civility. Bodhidharma, who brought Zen from India to China, is often referred to as a Barbarian since he was an Indian, or a foreigner in China. This term, when used in a Buddhist context, sometimes refers to the teaching of Zen, which is considered unorthodox or "foreign" to the traditional Buddhism that focused on scripture, scholarship and ritual practices.

JADE EMPEROR: The *Jade Emperor* is the ruler of the heavenly immortal beings, according to the mythology of Daoism.

KARMA: *Karma* means action. It also refers to the result of action, since the spiritual law of cause and effect states that the result is always preceded by causal action. Karma is sometimes misunderstood as a kind of fatalism, but the ultimate cause of all phenomena is the Mind, so mastery of the Mind begets mastery of karma.

KOAN: A *koan* is literally a public case, or a record of Zen dialogue. These dialogues are often used as means to test a student's realization. These dialogues can seem absurd, illogical or trivial and can generate a sense of bewilderment or doubt in the student's mind, which can only be resolved by transcending conventional thought and attachment.

LAND OF BLISS: See *Pure Land*.

LAO TZU: *Lao Tzu* was the founder of Daoism (or Taoism).

LAW OF CREATION: The *Law of Creation* is the principle concerning the manifestation of phenomenon.

MASTER LIN-JI: Zen *Master Lin-Ji* (787 - 867) is the founder of the Lin-Ji school of Zen, five generations after the Sixth Patriarch Hui-Neng. Lin-Ji approached his teacher, Master Huang-Bo, three times to ask for the true meaning of Buddha dharma. Each time, before he could even finish his sentence, he was hit by Huang-Bo. Discouraged, he took leave and went to Master Da-Yu and related his encounter. Da-Yu told him that Huang-Bo did it out of his motherly heart of kindness. Upon hearing this, *Lin-Ji* attained awakening and commented, "Huang-Bo's teaching is not so great!" Well-known for rigorous and intensive teaching style, *Master Lin-Ji* utilized the so-called four shouts and eight staffs as means for breaking student's attachment, no doubt due to the influence of his own awakening experience.

LOKAPALA: In Buddhism, *Lokapala* refers to the Four Guardian Spirits of the Four Cardinal Directions.

MASTER MA ZU: *Master Ma Zu* (709 - 788) was the second generation after the Sixth Patriarch Hui-Neng. Both the Lin-Ji school and Gui-Yan school of Zen can trace their lineage to Ma Zu (or Ma-Tzu).

MAHAYANA: *Mahayana,* one of the major schools Buddhism, literally means "great vehicle." Central to the *Mahayana* teaching is the concept of the Bodhisattva, for whom altruism is a key aspect of the spiritual path, being motivated by selfless compassion arising from the realization of the essential inseparability between himself and others. While other schools of Buddhism may not emphasize the ideal of a Bodhisattva path, it should be recognized that each path manifests according to the karma of the individual practitioner, just as different illness requires unique medicine to affect a cure. Practices that seem focused on liberating the practitioner's own suffering can also contribute significantly to the well-being of others. The merit of any path should only be judged within the context of the practitioner's unique situation in terms of its suitability to guide that individual toward the realization of the universal truth.

MANTRA: A sacred sound, either one syllable in a word or a set of words that have spiritual or mystical power, a *mantra* may have power to protect, purify, eliminate or magnify certain states of consciousness as well as to generate other effects. The power of a mantra comes from the pure function of the Mind, which is evoked by the repetition of the mantra.

MEDICINE BUDDHA: Known as the King of Lapis Lazuli Light, *Medicine Buddha* made, according to the sutra description, twelve vows to liberate sentient beings. Among the vows are to heal beings with deformities, illness and mental afflictions, and to awaken all beings through the lapis lazuli light.

MERIT: *Merit* is often considered to be the positive force that leads to desirable results in our life experience. More precisely, merit is the difference in the reality manifested by the Mind due to an elevated state of spiritual attainment.

MID-AUTUMN FESTIVAL: The *Mid-Autumn Festival* is a Chinese festival that occurs on the fifteenth of August on the lunar calendar, which corresponds to the day when the moon is fullest and roundest. This festival can be traced to moon worshiping in ancient China. The full moon is also a symbol for wholesomeness and often used in Zen teaching to indicate the Primordial Mind.

MIND DHARMA: *Mind dharma* is the aspect of Buddhist teachings that directly address the nature of the Mind.

MIND GROUND: The Mind can be described in terms of its essence, form and functions. *Mind Ground* refers to the essence aspect of the Mind.

MONKEY KING: *The Monkey King* is the main character in the Chinese classic novel *Journey to the West.* In the story, *the Monkey King* is the ruler of Mount

Flower and Fruit but becomes the disciple of a great Buddhist master (see Tang Sanzang) who vows to make the treacherous trip to India on foot in order to bring back more scriptures. While the story can be read as a magical fantasy, it can also be understood as a parable for the way the mind works. *The Monkey King* represents the restless aspect of the mind, or "monkey mind," of unenlightened beings. One of the powers of *The Monkey King* is his ability to manifest seventy-two transformations—thus symbolizing the quick, flexible and creative nature of the mind.

MOUNT FLOWER AND FRUIT: See Monkey King.

NEW AGE PHILOSOPHY: *New Age Philosophy* is the philosophical view that emerges from the New Age movement, which began in the 1960s. This movement is characterized by its rejection of traditional dogmatism and the embrace of alternative spiritual concept from the East. It emphasized the idea of "oneness" and social/religious inclusiveness.

ONE COMPOSITE: The physical world is *"one composite,"* since it is an entity that emerges through the composition of many elements. Our physical-psychological being is also described as *one composite,* as it is a collection of physical and psychological phenomena, namely the physical form (body), feelings, perceptions, volitions and consciousness.

NIRVANA: *Nirvana* is an eternal state of liberation whereby the suffering of cyclic birth and death ends both on the gross level of the physical body, or on the subtle level of moment-to-moment manifestation and disappearance of phenomena. Liberation from birth and death does not negate the nature of phenomena. Instead, it frees the practitioner from attachment to phenomena as something permanent so that the changing nature of phenomena no longer causes fundamental struggle or suffering within.

PEACH OF IMMORTALITY: In Chinese mythology, the *peach of immortality* is a heavenly fruit that brings longevity to the immortals or heavenly beings.

PLATFORM SUTRA: The *Platform Sutra* contains a recorded biography and account of the life and teaching of the Sixth Patriarch of Zen, Hui-Neng. The title of this book is based on the opening verse of this sutra: The Awakened Self Nature; Primordially Pure It Is; Just Use This Mind; Directly Actualize Buddhahood.

This sutra contains the wisdom and essence of early Zen teaching in China. When it was written, its highly accessible language pointed out the formless truth that underlies all existence, dispelled many common misunderstandings of classical scripture, and revealed the true purpose behind various forms of popular religious practices. Over time, this sutra has remained highly relevant to modern society as spiritual seekers attempt to cut through various presentations and discover the real message.

POET BAI (OR LI BAI): *Li Bai* (701 - 762) is considered one of the greatest poets in Chinese history. His poetry is characterized by its spontaneity and influence of Taoism and Zen. He was also referred to as the Poet Transcendent or the Retired Scholar of Azure Lotus. One of his most famous poems is called "Drinking Along Under Moonlight" and has been translated into English.

PRAJNA: The direct translation of *Prajna,* a sanskrit term, is "wisdom." In Buddhism, this word means the wisdom that transcends dualism. The mind that is trapped in duality engages in discursive thoughts and discrimination, whereas the pure mind is able to shine light on the totality of reality and see it as it truly is. It is through the pure mind that wisdom—or true understanding—arises because there is no distortion of reality. The Buddha advised his disciples to always rely on wisdom, not on the discrimination that is the typical state of unenlightened mind.

PRIMORDIAL MIND: Pure Mind or Innate Mind. It refers to the uncontaminated and unobstructed nature of the Mind, which is the origin and source of all existence.

PURE LAND: The pure living environment manifested by a Buddha through the pure function of the Mind is the *pure land.* The power of his vows makes each Buddha's pure land unique in its characteristics as well as the manifestation of an idealized environment for facilitating his own spiritual practice. Practitioners of Pure Land Buddhism purify their minds and vow to take rebirth after death in the Buddha's pure land in order to further his spiritual practice. Because the mind and our physical environment are inseparable aspects of the same essence, the Pure Land practice is essentially the practice of purifying the mind.

SAKYAMUNI: Sakya (or Shakya) is the Buddha's clan of origin in northern India, near the foothills of the Himalayas in present-day Nepal. The historical Buddha, known as *Sakyamuni* (Sage of the Sakya) Buddha (563 - 483 BCE), was born a prince. He abandoned a life of wealth, power and luxury in order to pursue a spiritual journey on which he sought to resolve the problems of the inevitable suffering of birth, death, illness and aging that he observed when venturing outside the protective environment of his palace.

SAMSARA: The cycles of birth, death and rebirth in the world of appearance are referred to as *samsara*. In Buddhist cosmology, *samsara* is typically described as six different states of existence determined by a person's accumulated habitual tendencies and dominant *karma*. In brief, these six realms are: heavenly being, human, jealous god, hungry ghost, animal and hell-being.

Rebirth as a heavenly being is due to a predominance of compassion, loving kindness, sympathetic joy, and equanimity in consciousness and actions. Being reborn as a jealous god occurs due to causes such as charitable actions conducted with regret or impure motivation that lead to material abundance but a strongly felt sense of dissatisfaction and jealousy. Existence as a human being is the result of mixed positive and negative thought, speech and action, none of which is very strong. The hungry ghost state is characterized by greed and craving; the animal realm is dominated by a lack of awareness and delusion; and reincarnation as a hell-being is caused by negative afflictions, such as anger or actions (such as killing) carried out with strong intent and accumulated force.

Samsara can also be understood as a metaphor of our moment-to-moment state of consciousness. The moment a person gives rise to compassion in the mind, that individual manifests the heavenly being's existence on earth. The very next moment, the arising of greed can manifest the mode of being of a hungry ghost. From this perspective, rebirth in a different realm does not simply occur after physical death but is instead the process of the moment-to-moment manifestation of the mind's function.

SENTIENT BEINGS: In Buddhism, the term *sentient being* is used to define all beings able to have a conscious experience of feelings and perception.

SHEN XIU: *Shen Xiu* was a contemporary of the Sixth Patriarch Hui-Neng and the leading disciple of the Fifth Patriarch. To show his understanding to the Fifth Patriarch, he composed the following verse:

> The body is a Bodhi tree,
>
> The mind is a clear standing mirror.
>
> Diligently and constantly we shall polish it,
>
> Let not a single dust settle.

In response, the Sixth Patriarch, an illiterate laborer in the monastery who had never attended even one teaching by the Fifth Patriarch, uttered this verse:

Bodhi has no tree in essence,

A clear mirror is not a stand either.

Since the beginning there was not a single thing,

From where could any dust come?

While Hui-Neng's verse demonstrated profound insight into the formless essence of reality, *Shen Xiu's* verse is still great advice for all spiritual practitioners. Through diligent practice, *Shen Xiu* later attained enlightenment as well. Because the Sixth Patriarch moved to Southern China to spread his teaching while *Shen Xiu* moved to the North, sometimes people refer to Hui-Neng's teaching as the Southern School and *Shen Xiu's* teaching as the Northern School.

SHI: *Shi* is the first Chinese character in the phonetic transliteration of the Buddha's name "Sakyamuni." As a Chinese custom, every Buddhist monastic adopted this character as his or her "family name" to symbolize the departure from worldly roles and responsibilities and entrance into the family of the Buddha.

SIXTH PATRIARCH: *Sixth Patriarch* Hui-Neng (638 - 713 BCE), regarded as the most important figure in Zen Buddhism, was instrumental in the wide propagation of Zen practice in China and later in Japan and Korea. All five schools of Zen Buddhism can trace their lineage to Hui-Neng. His teaching, as recorded in the Platform Sutra, is the most important source of early Zen teaching.

MASTER SHI TOU: (700 - 790) Three of the five Zen schools can trace their origins to *Shi-Tou* Xi-Qian, who lived two generations after the Sixth Patriarch Hui-neng.

SIX BODHISATTVA PRACTICES: The *Six Bodhisattva Practices* are generosity, morality, patience, effort, concentration and wisdom.

SUTRAS: *Sutras* are Buddhist scriptures that contain teachings of the Buddha.

TANG SANZANG: *Tang Sanzang* is an honorific title given to Xuanzang, the revered Buddhist monk scholar who traveled on foot from China to India and brought back many Buddhist scriptures and translations. His story has been famously adopted in the classic Chinese novel, *Journey to the West*. *Tang* refers to the ruling dynasty at that time (Tang Dynasty: 618 - 907). The term *Sanzang* means the Three Treasuries, which refers to the Collection of Buddhist teachings categorized as Sutra (recorded teaching of the Buddhist), Code of Discipline and Abidharmma (treatises on Buddha's teachings). A monastic who has mastered the understanding and practice of all three aspects of the teaching is given this honorific title. Because of the popularity and respect for Xuanzang, people usually refer to him simply by his title.

TAO: See Dao.

TEN DIRECTIONS: *Ten directions* (of space) is a Buddhist cosmological concept including the north, south, east, west, up, down, northwest, northeast, southeast and southwest.

TENDAI: *Tendai* (Chinese Tentai) is a philosophical school of Buddhism that became prominent during the Tang Dynasty. *Tendai* is based on the teaching of the Lotus Sutra.

THERAVADA: *Theravada* literally means "teaching of the elder," *Theravada* is the oldest school of Buddhism. Presently, it is practiced predominantly in Sri Lanka and Southeast Asia.

THREE PITIFUL TRANSMIGRATIONS: The *Three Pitiful Transmigrations* are the hell realm, hungry ghost realm and animal realm. Out of the six realms in which sentient beings can be reincarnated due to karma, these three are dominated by acute suffering. The hell realm is predominantly the karmic result of anger and hatred; the hungry ghost realm resonates mostly with greed, and the animal realm relates in general to a predominance of ignorance and lack of wisdom. Another way to understand these three realms is to understand them experientially in our daily life instead of that of a specific destination in future life. For example, when one is plagued by obsessive greed and insatiable desire, one's inner experience is similar to that of hunger and craving for an external source of satisfaction; metaphorically, one is already experiencing the hungry ghost realm even as a human being. All six realms of reincarnations can be understood this way. The principle of karma tells us that our rebirth in the next life will be determined by our strongest habitual tendencies. Therefore, it is possible for one to determine which realm one will reincarnate into by becoming aware of which afflictive emotion is the strongest in one's life: anger/hatred, ignorance or greed. Of course if one is able to cultivate and strengthen kindness, compassion, sympathetic joy and

The Origin Is Pure

equanimity, there is a possibility of escaping from the three pitiful realms and being reborn as a heavenly being. The causal condition for a human rebirth is that of a mixture of both positive and negative karma created through both beneficial and harmful thoughts, speech and actions, none of which is too strong to cause a fall to the pitiful states nor an ascension to the heavenly realm.

THIRD PATRIARCH SENG-CAN (or XUN-CAN, SENG-TSAN): The *Third Patriarch* of Zen lived in the sixth century CE. The poem "Faith in Mind" is attributed to him. This poem has been quoted extensively by past and present-day Zen masters in their teachings and writings. The poem opens this way:

> The ultimate Way is not difficult at all,
> Except your picking and choosing.
> Just stop craving and hatred,
> Then you will thoroughly understand.

TIBETAN BUDDHISM: The form of Buddhism practiced in Tibet. As Buddhism spread throughout Asia, it incorporated elements of indigenous religion as a skillful means of spreading the same spiritual message of the Buddha. Therefore, the custom and rituals of *Tibetan Buddhism* share similarities with the Bon religion. *Tibetan Buddhism* is also categorized as Vajrayana, the Diamond Vehicle, which incorporates the principles and practice of Tantra, which in turn means bringing awareness into that which is deluded. However, the Vajrayana teaching originated in India and is also practiced in various forms throughout China and Japan. One rather unique aspect of Tibetan Buddhism is the explicit identification of young children as reincarnated teachers or accomplished masters. These special individuals, referred to as Tulkus, are given systematic, rigorous religious training in order enssure the continuation of spiritual teaching and practices. The most prominent example is the current Dalai Lama, who is the fourteenth reincarnation of the same spiritual being who has been given the training and the roles as the religious leader of the Tibetan people in general.

TRIYANA: The *Triyana* are the three vehicles of Buddhism, namely Hinayana (Theravada), Mahayana and Vajrayana. They represent three different paths toward the same truth and differ by their emphasis in the method of practice.

VAIROCANA: The *Vairocana* Buddha is a historical Buddha whose name means "that which illuminates everything." Both the term and the Buddha refer to emptiness, or the essence of the Mind.

VAJRAYANA: *Vajrayana,* the Diamond Vehicle, is also known as Tantric Buddhism. It is an extension of Mahayana Buddhism and similar in philosophical aspects, but because it incorporates additional esoteric techniques to achieve enlightenment, some practices can only be transmitted in person by a qualified spiritual teacher under prescribed conditions.

VEXATION: Mental suffering that arises due to the gap between reality and our subjective perception of it is referred to as *vexation.*

WEI TUO: A protective deity of a Buddhist monastery in the traditional Mahayana system. *Wei Tuo* Bodhisattva has vowed to protect the minds of the spiritual practitioner from temptation and to maintain the harmony among the Sangha.

MASTER WEN YI: *Master Wen Yi* (885 - 958), Fayan *Wen Yi* played a critical role in establishing the Fayan School of Zen.

WESTERN PARADISE: *Western Paradise* typically refers to the Pure Land of Amida Buddha.

MASTER ZHAO ZHOU: See Elder Zhao Zhou.